U.S.-Cuban Relations in the 21st Century

Report of an Independent Task Force
Sponsored by the
Council on Foreign Relations

Bernard W. Aronson and William D. Rogers
Co-Chairs

The Council on Foreign Relations, Inc., a nonprofit, nonpartisan national membership organization founded in 1921, is dedicated to promoting understanding of international affairs through the free and civil exchange of ideas. The Council's members are dedicated to the belief that America's peace and prosperity are firmly linked to that of the world. From this flows the mission of the Council: to foster America's understanding of its fellow members of the international community, near and far, their peoples, cultures, histories, hopes, quarrels, and ambitions; and thus to serve, protect, and advance America's own global interests through study and debate, private and public.

THE COUNCIL TAKES NO INSTITUTIONAL POSITION ON POLICY ISSUES AND HAS NO AFFILIATION WITH THE U.S. GOVERNMENT. ALL STATEMENTS OF FACT AND EXPRESSIONS OF OPINION CONTAINED IN ALL ITS PUBLICATIONS ARE THE SOLE RESPONSIBILITY OF THE AUTHOR OR AUTHORS.

The Council on Foreign Relations will sponsor an Independent Task Force when (1) an issue of current and critical importance to U.S. foreign policy arises, and (2) it seems that a group diverse in backgrounds and perspectives may, nonetheless, be able to reach a meaningful consensus on a policy through private and nonpartisan deliberations. Typically, a Task Force meets between two and five times over a brief period to ensure the relevance of its work.

Upon reaching a conclusion, a Task Force issues a report, and the Council publishes its text and posts it on the Council's website. Task Force Reports can take three forms: (1) a strong and meaningful policy consensus, with Task Force members endorsing the general policy thrust and judgments reached by the group, though not necessarily every finding and recommendation; (2) a report stating the various policy positions, each as sharply and fairly as possible; or (3) a "Chairman's Report," where Task Force members who agree with the Chairman's Report may associate themselves with it, while those who disagree may submit dissenting statements. Upon reaching a conclusion, Task Forces may also ask individuals who were not members of the Task Force to associate themselves with the Task Force Report to enhance its impact. All Task Force Reports "benchmark" their findings against current administration policy in order to make explicit areas of agreement and disagreement. The Task Force is solely responsible for its report. The Council takes no institutional position.

For further information about the Council or this Task Force, please write the Council on Foreign Relations, 58 East 68th Street, New York, NY 10021, or call the Director of Communications at (212) 434-9400. Visit our website at www.foreignrelations.org.

CONTENTS

FOREWORD

Forty years after Fidel Castro's seizure of power, the United States and Cuba remain deeply estranged, and U.S. policy toward Cuba continues to excite debate pro and con here and abroad. Some observers expected rapid change in relations between the United States and Cuba at the end of the Cold War. Some thought that, deprived of support from the Soviet Union, the Castro regime would have to introduce sweeping economic and political changes to survive—and might well collapse as did so many communist regimes in 1989–90. Others expected that whatever happened in Cuba, U.S. policy toward the island would change once its relationship with Cuba was no longer a part of the great global contest with the Soviet Union.

Ten years after the end of the Cold War, however, the political situation in Cuba and U.S. policy toward Havana are only slightly changed. Despite a precipitous economic decline, Fidel Castro's government remains committed to building state socialism. Cuba's economic reforms—allowing dollars to circulate freely on the island, opening farmers' markets to supplement the state distribution system, and permitting the very modest growth of self-employment—have not altered the basic structure of the Cuban economic system. Politically, Cuba is still a one-party state, and independent and well-respected human rights organizations regularly identify serious human rights abuses on the island.

U.S. policy toward Cuba has also remained remarkably unchanged in the aftermath of the Cold War. However, the rationale for U.S. policy toward the island has changed—from opposing Cuba's efforts to support armed, pro-Soviet revolutionary groups in the region to opposing Cuba's domestic record on human rights and lack of democracy—but the economic embargo first proclaimed by President Kennedy in 1962 remains the centerpiece of U.S. policy.

Because of what has changed and not changed, the time seems ripe for a fresh look at U.S. policy toward Cuba. With the United States less interested in containing communism than in promoting democracy, Cuba may still pose problems for policymakers, but they are not the same problems that the United States faced in the Cold War. After 40 years, the long era of Fidel Castro's personal rule in Cuba is also drawing to a close. These considerations raise the question of whether the United States should begin to focus less on dealing with President Castro and think more about its long-term relationship with the Cuban people.

In this context, the Council on Foreign Relations, while not taking a position as an institution, sponsored a bipartisan Independent Task Force on U.S.-Cuban Relations in the 21st Century. Task Force members engaged in a comprehensive policy review, identifying U.S. interests with respect to Cuba now and in the future, evaluating current policy, and crafting a range of recommendations that can be implemented within the framework of current legislation.

The Task Force was chaired jointly by Bernard W. Aronson and William D. Rogers, both former assistant secretaries of state for inter-American affairs. Its distinguished members included widely respected scholars, legal analysts, businesspeople, and former government officials representing a broad range of views and backgrounds. A number of congressional and White House staff members participated in the Task Force meetings as observers. In addition to the members of the Task Force and the listed observers, the Task Force sought comments and advice from a wide variety of experts and interested persons, holding meetings in Atlanta, Houston, Miami, Chicago, and Los Angeles. A delegation was also sent to the Vatican, where members and staff met with Pope John Paul II and with senior Vatican officials to receive their comments on the draft report.

Meeting on three occasions in the fall of 1998, the Task Force decided to look for what it considered to be new and flexible policy approaches toward Cuba based on the new conditions shaping the relationship. While the Task Force did not recommend an end to the embargo or a normalization of official diplomatic relations between the two countries, the group studied a variety of measures that, in its judgment, would tend to normalize relations between the Cuban and American people now and lay the groundwork for better official relations in the future. The Task Force favors a bipartisan policy toward Cuba. At the same time, the Task Force recognized that the president retains very broad authority to modify existing policy toward Cuba, and most of its recommendations call for presidential action, rather than new legislation.

The Task Force members, many of whom have played an active part in formulating recent policy toward Cuba, endorsed a wide variety of measures suggested by the co-chairs in relation to the Cuban American community. Members also supported expanding people-to-people contact through travel and other exchanges, facilitating the delivery of food and medicine to the island, promoting direct American private-sector investment, and stepping up cooperation with Cuba where specific U.S. interests are involved. Notably, the co-chairs and the Task Force members chose not to condition their recommendations on changes in Cuban policy. Whatever Castro does, the Task Force concluded, it is in the interest of the United States to promote broad contacts and engagement between the American and Cuban people and, as the need arises, to provide humanitarian assistance to our neighbors.

Finally, I would like to thank Bernard Aronson and William Rogers, the co-chairs of the Task Force, for their steadfast leadership; Walter Mead and Julia Sweig, the project director and program coordinator, respectively, for their hard and good work in seeing that the Task Force ran smoothly; and Council members for raising important questions on the subject. Most of all, thanks are due to the Task Force itself, for stimulating debate on an issue that requires more serious attention.

Leslie H. Gelb
President
Council on Foreign Relations

ACKNOWLEDGMENTS

Over the past six months, the Independent Task Force on U.S.-Cuban Relations in the 21st Century sponsored by the Council on Foreign Relations has benefited from the assistance of many individuals. The success of this Task Force is due in large measure to the leadership provided by its co-chairs, Bernard W. Aronson and William D. Rogers. I am especially indebted to the members and observers of the Task Force, who offered their wisdom, intellect, and experience during the crafting of this report. In addition, the report and activities of the Task Force have benefited from comments provided by Professors Jorge Domínguez, Marifeli Pérez-Stable, María de los Angeles Torres, Carmelo Mesa-Lago, and Damian Fernández, as well as from former White House adviser for Cuba, Richard Nuccio.

The Task Force also benefited from a series of meetings and discussions set up through the Council's National Program and its partner institutes. These meetings were of great value in that they enabled the Task Force to take account of the views of people outside the Washington–New York circuit. The Task Force Report underwent many changes between the first draft and the final report. Many of these were due to the extremely helpful—and sometimes quite pointed—suggestions and comments we received in the national meetings. I would like to thank all those who took the time to review the report and attend these meetings, and thank the Pacific Council on International Policy in Los Angeles, the Carter Center in Atlanta, the Chicago Council on Foreign Relations, the James A. Baker III Institute for Public Policy of Rice University in Houston, and the Dante B. Fascell North-South Center of the University of Miami for hosting us so generously and graciously.

Special thanks are due also to those who enabled the Task Force to confer with senior Vatican officials. His Eminence Bernard Cardinal Law, archbishop of Boston, arranged our participation in an audience with His Holiness Pope John Paul II and a meeting with His Excellency Most Reverend Jean Louis Tauran, Vatican secretary for relations with states. The generosity of Allen Adler made the visit possible.

At the Council on Foreign Relations we would like to acknowledge the support for the Task Force provided by Nelson and David Rockefeller Senior Fellow for Inter-American Studies and Director of the Latin America Program Kenneth R. Maxwell, Vice President for Corporate Affairs and Publisher David Kellogg, Director of Publishing Patricia Dorff, Director of Communications April Wahlestedt, Vice President and Director of the Council's Washington Program Paula J. Dobriansky, and Assistant Director of the Council's Washington Program Lorraine G. Snyder.

I also want to thank my colleagues on the Task Force staff without whom this report could not have been written. First and foremost, Senior Program Coordinator Julia Sweig provided hard work, intellectual leadership, and commitment without which both our process and our product would have been much poorer. Additionally, my research associate Rebecca O'Brien and intern Benjamin Skinner went far beyond the call of duty to provide the Task Force with seamless research and administrative support from New York. I am also grateful to Kaya Adams whose administrative support in Washington greatly facilitated our work.

I would like to express gratitude to the Arthur Ross Foundation and the Open Society Institute, whose contributions provided financial support for this Task Force.

Walter Russell Mead
Project Director
Council on Foreign Relations

INTRODUCTION

In reviewing U.S. policy toward Cuba, this Task Force is well aware that we are undertaking one of the most difficult and perhaps thankless tasks in American foreign policy. Our domestic debate about Cuba has been polarized and heated for decades, but this report seeks to build new common ground and consensus with hope and confidence. What shapes our recommendations is a sense that U.S.-Cuban relations are entering a new era. We have tried to analyze the nature of this new era, understand the American national interest vis-à-vis Cuba at this time, and develop an approach to Cuba policy that avoids the polarization of the past.

We have not tackled every outstanding issue. Instead, we have elected to try to break the current logjam by proposing new steps that we hope can elicit broad bipartisan support. Some will find our recommendations too conservative; others will argue that our proposals will strengthen the current Cuban regime. We hope and trust, instead, that these proposals will promote U.S. interests and values by hastening the day when a fully democratic Cuba can reassume a friendly, normal relationship with the United States.

Too often, discussions of U.S. policy toward Cuba start from the position that the policy over the last four decades has been a failure. Both opponents and supporters of the embargo sometimes embrace this conclusion as a starting point and then urge either jettisoning the embargo because it is counterproductive and a failure, or tightening the embargo to increase its effectiveness.

We believe that U.S. policy toward Cuba throughout the Cold War sought to achieve many goals, ranging from the overthrow of the current regime to the containment of the Soviet empire. Not all these goals were achieved. Cuba remains a highly repressive regime where the basic human rights and civil liberties of the Cuban people are routinely denied and repressed. Indeed, in its annual report issued in December 1998, Human Rights Watch said that Cuba has experienced "a disheartening return to heavy-handed repression." Still, we believe that U.S. policy toward Cuba, including the embargo, has enjoyed real, though not total, success.

The dominant goal of U.S. policy toward Cuba during the Cold War was to prevent the advance of Cuban-supported communism in this hemisphere as part of an overall global strategy of containing Soviet communism. There was a time in this hemisphere when the danger of Cuban-style communism threatened many nations in Latin America, when many young people, academics, and intellectuals looked to Cuba as a political and economic model, and when Cuban-supported violent revolutionary groups waged war on established governments from El Salvador to Uruguay.

That time is gone, and no informed observer believes it will reappear. Cuban communism is dead as a potent political force in the Western Hemisphere. Democracy is ascendant in the Western Hemisphere, however fragile and incomplete it remains in some nations. Today, electoral democracy is considered the only legitimate form of government by the member states of the Organization of American States (OAS), and they are formally committed to defend it.

A 1998 Defense Intelligence Agency analysis concluded that Cuba no longer poses a threat to our national security. Cuba's Caribbean neighbors are normalizing their relations with Cuba not because they fear Cuban subversion, but in part because they understand that Cuban ideological imperialism no longer constitutes a regional force. The emergence of democracy throughout the hemisphere, the loss of Soviet support, sustained U.S. pressure, and Cuba's own economic woes forced the Cuban regime to renounce its support of armed revolutionary groups. Containment has succeeded, and the era when it needed to be the organizing principle of U.S. foreign policy toward Cuba has ended.

Throughout the Cold War the United States sought either to induce Fidel Castro to introduce democratic political reforms or to promote his replacement as head of the Cuban state. We believe support for democracy should be our central goal toward Cuba. But we also believe that the time has come for the United States to move beyond its focus on Fidel Castro, who at 72 will not be Cuba's leader forever, and to concentrate on supporting, nurturing, and strengthening the civil society that is slowly, tentatively, but persistently beginning to emerge in Cuba beneath the shell of Cuban communism.

This is not a repudiation of our policy of containment but its natural evolution. As George F. Kennan wrote, containment was not simply a strategy to limit the influence of communism in the world. In his 1947 *Foreign Affairs* article, Kennan argued that communism, as an economic system, required the continuous conquest of new resources and populations to survive. Once bottled up, communist systems will decay. Its poor economic performance and its frustration of the natural human desire for freedom make communism a doomed system if it cannot expand. Communism's collapse across Eastern Europe and the Soviet Union triumphantly vindicated Kennan's views.

The processes of decay that Kennan foresaw for the Soviet Union after containment are already far advanced in Cuba. The Cuban economy contracted significantly after Soviet subsidies ended. Cuba has legalized the dollar, tolerated modest small-business development, however limited, and sought foreign investment in tourism to attract desperately needed foreign exchange.

The Cuban government's formidable instruments of repression keep open dissenters marginalized, but the poverty and repression of daily life for most Cubans, combined with the affluence they see among foreign tourists and Cubans with access to hard currency, are steadily eating away at the foundations of Cuba's system. Pope John Paul II's extraordinary visit to Cuba in January 1998 revealed a deep spiritual hunger in Cuba and massive popular support for the Cuban church. The regime has lost the struggle for the hearts and minds of Cuba's youth, few of whom long for a future under Cuban-style "socialism." Indeed, we believe that in both civil society and, increasingly, within middle-level elements of the Cuban elite, many Cubans understand that their nation must undergo a profound transformation to survive and succeed in the new globalized economy and in today's democratic Western Hemisphere.

Cubans on the island also know well that while they remain citizens of an impoverished nation, struggling to meet the daily necessities of life more than 40 years after the revolution, Cubans and Cuban Americans one hundred miles to the north are realizing great economic and professional achievements. This peaceful majority of Cuban Americans in the United States, by demonstrating that freedom, capitalism, and respect for human dignity can allow ordinary people to achieve their full potential, is helping erode the Cuban regime's domestic credibility.

Almost every person in Cuba knows someone who lives in the United States. Increased contact between Cubans on the island and their friends and relations in the United States—a central goal of U.S. policy since the 1992 passage of the Cuban Democracy Act— may have done more to weaken the Cuban government than any other single factor since the collapse of the Soviet Union.

While it is by no means clear how fast change will come in Cuba, there is no doubt that change will come. The regime has two choices. Both lead to change. On the one hand, it can open up to market forces, allowing more Cubans to open small businesses and inviting more foreign investment to build up the economy. This will relieve Cuba's economic problems to some extent—with or without a change in U.S. policy—but at the cost of undermining the ideological basis of the Cuban system.

The alternative—to throttle Cuban small business and keep foreign investment to a minimum—also will not preserve the status quo in Cuba. If Cuba refuses to accept further economic reforms, its economy will continue to decay, and popular dissatisfaction with the system will increase. Just as Kennan predicted 50 years ago in the Soviet case, a communist system forced to live on its own resources faces inevitable change.

U.S. opposition to Cuban-supported revolution and U.S. support for democracy and development in this hemisphere played critical roles in frustrating Cuba's ambitions to extend its economic model and political influence. With this success in hand, the United States can now turn to the second stage of its long-term policy on Cuba: working to create the best possible conditions for a peaceful transition in Cuba and the emergence of a democratic, prosperous, and free Cuba in the 21st century.

A look at postcommunist Europe shows us that the end of communism can lead to many different results—some favorable, others not so favorable. In Poland, the Czech Republic, and Hungary, the end of communism started a process of democratic and economic development. In contrast, new governments in much of the former Soviet Union are ineffective and corrupt. Criminal syndicates dominate some of these new economies, and ordinary people have suffered catastrophic declines in living standards. In Nicaragua, free elections ended Sandinista rule, but the successor governments have not yet put the country on the path to prosperity.

Furthermore, there are many different ways in which communist regimes can change. In the former Czechoslovakia, the "Velvet Revolution" led to a peaceful transfer of power. In Romania, the former ruler and his wife died in a bloody internal struggle.

In Poland, civil society developed within the shell of communism, enabling Solidarity to strike a bargain with the Communist Party that provided for a limited period of power-sharing prior to truly free and fair elections. During this transition, the United States—both the government and many nongovernmental organizations—actively engaged with and supported Poland's emerging civil society, from the Catholic Church and human rights groups to the Polish trade union movement. Simultaneously, while the U.S. government directly supported Poland's emerging civil society, it also offered the carrot of relaxing existing sanctions to persuade the military regime to release political prisoners and open space for free expression of ideas and political activity.

As a unique society with its own history and social dynamics, Cuba will find its own solution to the problem posed by its current government. The United States cannot ordain how Cuba will make this change, but U.S. policy should create conditions that encourage and support a rapid, peaceful, democratic transition.

The United States has learned something else about transitions. Some who formerly served the old regimes, whether through conviction, opportunism, or necessity, have become credible and constructive members of the newly emerging democratic governments and societies. The Polish armed forces—which enforced martial law against Solidarity in the early 1980s—are now a trusted NATO partner. Throughout Central and Eastern Europe and the former Soviet Union, officials who once served the communist system became valuable, democratic-minded members of new, free societies. Some former communist parties reorganized themselves on democratic lines in Italy as well as in Eastern and Central Europe—and now play key roles as center-left parties in constitutional democracies.

This experience allows the United States to approach Cuba today with more flexibility than in the past. Some who today serve the Cuban government as officials may well form part of a democratic transition tomorrow. Indeed, enabling and encouraging supporters of the current system to embrace a peaceful democratic transition would significantly advance both U.S. and Cuban interests in the region.

The American national interest would be poorly served if Cuba's transition led to widespread chaos, internal violence, divisive struggles over property rights, increased poverty, and social unrest on the island. An additional danger for the United States would arise if chaos and instability led to uncontrolled mass migration into the United States. Having tens or hundreds of thousands of desperate Cubans fleeing across the Florida Straits would create both humanitarian and political emergencies for the United States. Civil strife in Cuba would also have serious consequences for the United States, including potential pressures for the United States to intervene militarily.

On the other hand, the benefits to the United States of a peaceful, democratic, and prosperous Cuba would be substantial. A democratic Cuba has the potential to be a regional leader in the Caribbean in the fight against drug trafficking and money laundering. As a trading partner, Cuba would be a significant market for U.S. agricultural, industrial, and high-tech goods and services. A reviving tourist industry in Cuba will create tens of thousands of jobs in the United States. Working together, the United States, Cuba, and other countries in the region can protect endangered ecosystems such as the Caribbean's coral reefs, cooperate on air/sea rescues and hurricane prediction, and develop new plans for regional integration and economic growth.

Finally, the growth of a stable democratic system in Cuba will permit the resumption of the friendship between Cubans and U.S. citizens, a friendship that has immeasurably enriched the culture of both countries. The estrangement between Cuba and the United States is painful for both countries; a return to close, friendly, and cooperative relations is something that people of good-will in both countries very much want to see.

TASK FORCE RECOMMENDATIONS
AND CURRENT POLICY

With the end of the Cold War, substantial strains on the Cuban economy, and the end of Cuban support for armed revolutionary movements in the Western Hemisphere, U.S. policy toward Cuba has evolved through the 1990s. The 1992 Cuban Democracy Act (CDA) both strengthened economic sanctions against the Castro regime and authorized the president to implement a range of measures to promote exchanges and contacts between Americans and Cubans and take unspecified measures "to support the Cuban people." Following passage of the CDA, the administration reached an agreement with Cuba that restored direct phone service between the two countries, permitted the opening of news bureaus in Havana, and began to ease travel restrictions for scholars, artists, and others. At the same time, the CDA tightened the embargo by blocking trade between third-country U.S. subsidiaries and Cuba. In 1994 and 1995, the United States and Cuba signed immigration accords under whose terms 20,000 Cuban citizens are allowed to emigrate to the United States each year, including up to 5,000 Cubans per year who qualify as political refugees. Cubans attempting to enter the United States irregularly are returned to Cuba.

In 1996, following the downing by Cuban MiGs of two American planes and the deaths of three American citizens and one legal resident, the Cuban Liberty and Democratic Solidarity Act (popularly known as Helms-Burton) passed Congress and was signed into law by the president. The new law further defined U.S. policy toward Cuba. Title I seeks to strengthen international sanctions against the Cuban government through a variety of diplomatic measures. Title II delineates the conditions under which the president may provide direct assistance for and otherwise relate to a new or transitional government in Cuba.[1] Title III further internationalizes the embargo by exposing foreign investment in nationalized Cuban properties to the risk of legal challenge in U.S. courts by American citizens who formerly owned such property, including individuals who at the time of confiscation were Cuban nationals but who have since become U.S. citizens. A provision of the law allows the president to prevent legal action in the courts by exercising a waiver of Title III every six months. Title IV denies entry into the United States to executives (and their family members) of companies who invest in properties confiscated from persons who are now U.S. citizens.

In the aftermath of the 1996 attack on U.S. civilian planes, the administration tightened sanctions against Cuba, including suspending direct flights from Miami to Havana. The administration continued to exercise its semiannual waiver authority, preventing American citizens from taking legal action pursuant to Title III of Helms-Burton.

U.S. policy evolved following John Paul II's historic visit to Cuba in January 1998, as a bipartisan consensus began to emerge in the Congress and the executive to explore ways to increase the flow of humanitarian aid to the Cuban people. On March 20, 1998, the administration restored daily charter flights and renewed the right of Cuban Americans to send remittances to family members on the island. Tensions between the two countries remain, however. In September 1998 the United States arrested ten Cuban citizens in connection with an alleged spy ring operating in South Florida. In relation to those arrests, in December 1998 the United States expelled three diplomats at the Cuban mission to the United Nations.

In spite of these continuing problems, we favor increasing people-to-people contact between American and Cuban citizens and with Cuban civil society and further facilitating the donation

---

[1] The impact of Title II on U.S. policy is disputed. When the president signed Helms-Burton into law, he stated that, "consistent with the Constitution, I interpret the act as not derogating the president's authority to conduct foreign policy." Noting that Title II "could be read to state the foreign policy of the United States," he announced that he viewed the Title II provisions as "precatory," or as a petition by the Congress. Many congressional leaders do not support this view.

and distribution of humanitarian aid. Building on the provisions of existing law and policy that opened the doors to these wider contacts, our recommendations call for substantially stepped-up people-to-people contact and intensified and decentralized humanitarian relief efforts. We believe that beneath the surface of Cuban communism a modest transition has begun, both in the attitudes of many Cubans living on the island and in emerging church, civic, and small-scale private sector activities. Clearly, the challenge to U.S. policy is to encourage and support this inevitable transition.

FRAMEWORK OF RECOMMENDATIONS

While we no longer expect Cuban communism to survive indefinitely or spread, it should remain a clear objective of U.S. policy neither to support nor to appear to support the current regime. A broad, bipartisan consensus in the United States now exists that the U.S. government should use its influence to support democratic development throughout the Americas. This recognition is axiomatic in U.S. foreign policy and remains the cornerstone of U.S. efforts to promote regional economic integration. The Cuban dictatorship merits no exception to U.S. policy in the Western Hemisphere. This is the first principle that guided us in developing our recommendations:

No change in U.S. policy toward Cuba should have the primary effect of consolidating or legitimizing the status quo on the island. On the other hand, every aspect of U.S. foreign and economic policy toward Cuba should be judged by a very pragmatic standard: whether it contributes to rapid, peaceful, democratic change in Cuba while safeguarding the vital interests of the United States.

SUMMARY OF RECOMMENDATIONS

Our recommendations come in five baskets. Under "The Cuban American Community," we make proposals to increase contacts between Cuban Americans and their friends and families on the island. Under "The Open Door," we propose additional measures to increase contacts between U.S. and Cuban citizens and to open the windows and doors to the world that the current Cuban regime has nailed shut. Under "Humanitarian Aid," the third basket, we offer proposals to assist the victims of the Cuban regime, including both Cuban Americans and people still on the island. Our fourth basket, "The Private Sector," sets forth criteria for a gradual introduction of U.S. economic activities in Cuba to support the recommendations in the first three baskets of proposals. A fifth basket of "National Interest" recommendations makes specific proposals for addressing particular problems that involve U.S. national interests. In general, most of these changes can be initiated unilaterally by the United States and will not require bilateral negotiations with the Cuban regime. The Task Force proposals go well beyond current administration policy with respect to people-to-people contact and humanitarian aid. However, in the case of the private-sector recommendations, the full implementation of these proposals requires changes in Cuban policy and law.

Some of us would propose more sweeping changes, such as unilaterally lifting the embargo and all travel restrictions; others vehemently oppose this step. We do not dismiss these debates, but we chose in this report not to engage in them. U.S. policy must build a bipartisan consensus to be effective. Therefore, we have consciously sought new common ground.

RECOMMENDATIONS

BASKET ONE: THE CUBAN AMERICAN COMMUNITY

Cuban American remittances to friends, families, and churches in Cuba are estimated by various sources at between $400 million and $800 million annually. However measured, this is the island's largest single source of hard currency. While it is perfectly normal for developing countries to receive remittances, in the Cuban political context, the dependence on U.S. dollars sent home by Cuban Americans is a humiliating badge of failure. Cuba has become a charity case, dependent on handouts from those it has persecuted, oppressed, or driven away by poverty.

Some voices in the United States argue that, by enhancing hard-currency holdings in Cuba, remittances prop up the current regime and prolong the island's agony. This argument is not without merit, but, on balance, we disagree. First, we share a basic moral and humanitarian concern over easing the suffering of Cuba's people. Moreover, the success of the Cuban American community is one of the most powerful factors in promoting change in Cuba. The transfers of money, goods, and medical supplies from Cuban Americans to friends, family, and religious communities in Cuba are helping create a new group of Cubans who no longer depend on the state for their means of survival.

Remittances from Cuban Americans help create small businesses in Cuba and allow hundreds of thousands of Cubans to improve their lives independent of government control. Furthermore, Cuban Americans will play an important role in the construction of a postcommunist Cuba. Their national and global contacts, understanding of market economies, and professional skills will give them a vital role as a bridge between the United States and Cuba when Cuba rejoins the democratic community.

Cuban American Community Recommendations

1. End Restrictions on Humanitarian Visits. We recommend an end to all restrictions on the number of humanitarian visits that Cuban Americans are permitted to make each year. The federal government should not be the judge of how often Cuban Americans, or any other Americans, need to visit relatives living abroad.

2. Raise the Ceiling on Remittances. Under current regulations, only Cuban Americans are permitted to send up to $1,200 per year to family members on the island. We recommend that the ceiling on annual remittances be increased to $10,000 per household and that all U.S. residents with family members living in Cuba should be permitted to send remittances to their family members at this level on a trial basis for 18 months. This policy should continue if the executive, in consultation with Congress, concludes at the trial period's end that the Cuban regime has not enacted tax or other regulatory policies to siphon off a significant portion of these funds, and that this policy furthers the foreign policy interests of the United States.

3. Allow Retirement to Cuba for Cuban Americans. We recommend that retired and/or disabled Cuban Americans be allowed to return to Cuba if they choose, collecting Social Security and other pension benefits to which they are entitled in the United States, and be granted corresponding banking facilities.

4. Promote Family Reunification. Many members of the Cuban American community are concerned about the difficulty their family members in Cuba encounter in getting U.S. visas for family visits. While commending the efforts of the overworked consular staff in Havana, we believe it is important that Cuban Americans receive and be seen to receive fair and courteous treatment. We recommend that the State Department and Immigration and Naturalization Service (INS) make every effort in processing requests at the U.S. Interests Section in Havana to insure that Cuban citizens wishing to visit family members in the United States face no higher hurdle in obtaining visas

than that faced by family members in other countries wishing to visit relatives in this country. We recommend that State Department and INS officials meet regularly with representatives of the Cuban American community to discuss ways to expedite the determination of eligibility for family visits to the United States. Later in this report, we recommend an expansion of U.S. consular services in Cuba.

5. Restore Direct Mail Service. The 1992 Cuban Democracy Act grants the president the authority to authorize direct mail service between the United States and Cuba. We recommend that representatives of the U.S. and Cuban postal services meet to begin restoring direct mail service between the two countries.

BASKET TWO: THE OPEN DOOR

Since the passage of the 1992 Cuban Democracy Act, U.S. law has recognized that spreading accurate and fair information about the outside world in Cuba is an important goal of American foreign policy. The lack of information about events in Cuba has also enabled the Cuban regime to persecute its own people with little fear that foreigners will come to their support—or, in some cases, even know what the Cuban government is doing. Whether through Radio Martí, restoring direct telephone service, or promoting cultural and academic exchanges, the United States has consistently sought to increase the access of Cubans to news and information from abroad.

We believe the time has come to significantly upgrade and intensify these efforts. The Cuban people are hungry for American and world culture, for contacts with scholars and artists from other countries, for opportunities to study abroad, for new ideas and fresh perspectives. U.S. policy should encourage these exchanges and encounters through every available measure.

Recommendations

Open Door Recommendations

1. Facilitate Targeted Travel. Despite bureaucratic obstacles erected by both governments, the exchange of ideas remains one of the most promising areas for genuinely fruitful people-to-people contact. Since 1995, the United States has significantly cut the red tape surrounding academic exchanges. We commend that trend and urge the further reduction of restrictions on academic (undergraduate, graduate, and postgraduate) and other exchanges. We recommend that, following a one-time application, the Office of Foreign Assets Control (OFAC) grant a "permanent specific license" to all Americans with a demonstrable professional or other serious interest in traveling to Cuba for the purpose of engaging in academic, scientific, environmental, health, cultural, athletic, religious, or other activities. The presumption would be that these applications would normally and routinely receive approval.[2]

   In 1994, Congress passed a Sense of Congress resolution stating that "the president should not restrict travel or exchanges for informational, educational, religious, cultural or humanitarian purposes or for public performances or exhibitions between the United States and any other country." At the same time, congressional policy toward Cuba has increasingly focused on opening opportunities for meaningful encounters between American and Cuban citizens. Thus, we recommend that the OFAC grant easily renewable multiple-entry special licenses to travel agencies and nongovernmental organizations for structured travel programs available to groups and individuals for the purposes enumerated by Congress. Individual participants in such travel would visit Cuba under the organizing agency's license.

---

[2] Current regulations require all individuals wishing to travel to Cuba (with the exception of journalists who may travel without government preclearance under a "general license") to apply for a "specific license," for which applicants must demonstrate a preestablished legitimate professional or research interest in Cuba. Persons traveling under a "general license" to Cuba are not required to clear their plans with the U.S. government in advance. They are, however, required to certify at reentry to the United States that their travel and activities in Cuba conformed to the purposes for which the licenses are granted; making false statements is a violation of federal law.

This recommendation is formulated to facilitate a more open relationship between Cubans and Americans, not to support a Cuban tourism industry currently built on a system that prevents foreign employers from hiring and paying workers fairly and directly and denies Cuban citizens access to facilities designated exclusively for foreigners. When and if employers are able to hire and pay their workers directly, and when the system of "apartheid tourism" ends, we recommend that the United States consider permitting leisure travel.

2. Allow More Private Visits of Certain Cuban Officials to the United States. The United States currently denies visas for travel to the United States by Cuban officials who rank at the ministerial level and by the 500 deputies of the National Assembly of People's Power. Because of the positions they now hold and may assume in the future, many such individuals are among those we believe should have the opportunity to interact with Americans, to experience our system directly, and to witness the vigor and openness of our own public policy debate. We recommend that the United States lift its blanket ban on travel to the United States by deputies of the National Assembly and Cuban cabinet ministers, exercising a presumption of approval for applications from these officials for travel to the United States, except for those identified by the State Department who are credibly believed to have directly and personally participated in or ordered grave acts of repression that violate international law, or who represent a legitimate security concern to the United States. In making this recommendation we seek to encourage nongovernmental and private contacts such as those sponsored by U.S. academic institutions. We recognize that this recommendation risks greater penetration of the United States by Cuban intelligence agencies. We have confidence in the ability of U.S. national security agencies to guard against this threat, and we believe that the gains far outweigh the risks. Nevertheless, this danger must be carefully watched and adjustments in this policy calibrated accordingly.

3. Facilitate Cultural Collaboration and Performances by Americans in Cuba and by Cubans in the United States. Since the passage of the 1992 Cuban Democracy Act, there has been a significant increase in the number of Cuban artists, actors, and musicians traveling to the United States. Unfortunately, fewer U.S. performers have traveled to Cuba. These exchanges and activities are vital to any strategy to end the cultural isolation of the Cuban people. Through simplified visa and license procedures and other mechanisms, the U.S. government should encourage an increase in these programs. We applaud efforts to date to support such initiatives and recommend further that the United States encourage collaboration between American and Cuban artists and allow transactions for the creation of new cultural and/or artistic products. Cuban artists performing in the United States today are allowed to receive only modest per diem payments to cover living expenses. We recommend that Cuban artists performing in the United States be allowed to receive freely negotiated fees from their American hosts. Similarly, American artists performing in Cuba should be eligible to be paid for their work at reasonable negotiated rates.

4. Protect and Share Intellectual Property. Currently, Cuba systematically pirates significant amounts of U.S. cultural and intellectual property, ranging from Hollywood movies broadcast on Cuban television to computer software used throughout the island. Cuba refuses to consider paying for this illegal use of intellectual property, citing the U.S. embargo as an excuse. This creates an awkward situation for the United States. On the one hand, our interest in opening Cuba to outside influences leads us to encourage and even facilitate Cuba's access to U.S. and other foreign films, cultural materials, and political and economic literature. On the other hand, the U.S. government cannot condone theft from U.S. citizens and corporations. Furthermore, we must ensure that Cuba does not become an international center for the illegal production and redistribution of pirated intellectual property. We therefore propose that the United States allow and encourage U.S. companies and artists

to guarantee and protect their trademarks and copyrights and to negotiate permission for Cuba to use their products. We recommend that the U.S. government license and approve these transactions and authorize companies to spend funds obtained through these settlements for filming, recording, translation, or other legitimate cultural activities in Cuba. Likewise, we encourage both governments to regularize and comply with domestic and international trademark and copyright protection regimes.

5. Pioneer "Windows on the World." Successful transitions to multi-party systems and market and mixed market economies in Eastern Europe, Spain, Portugal, and Latin America may offer constructive guideposts to help Cuba's transition occur in as benign a manner as possible. To that end, the United States should pioneer the creation of a merit-based program for Cubans to study in American universities and technical training institutes. The program should also include sending professionals with technical expertise to advise Cuba in the development of institutional mechanisms that support the emergence of small businesses and private farms. In addition, we recommend that the United States Information Agency (USIA) invite Cuban government officials (except those excluded as defined in Basket Two, Item Two) and scholars for its programs that bring foreign citizens to meet with their peers in and out of government in the United States.

We further recommend that funds be made available from various public and independent sources, such as the National Endowment for the Arts, the National Endowment for Humanities, the National Endowment for Democracy, the Fulbright scholarship program, and from private foundations for university and other programs to support national, regional, and bilateral research activities involving Cuba. This includes support for new acquisitions by Cuban libraries. In addition, we recommend that the United States encourage and facilitate direct funding of in-country activities by private foundations so that their grant-making activities can include direct support to Cuban research institutions and community organizations. We recommend that the U.S. government consult with foundation officers and others with expertise in this field to determine a fair and feasible approach. We note with concern that some academic and other nongovernmental institutions, citing pressure from the Cuban government, have barred Cuban Americans from participating in existing exchange programs. Discrimination based on ethnicity or place of origin is a violation of U.S. civil rights laws. All organizations participating in exchanges or other activities with Cuba should state clearly that in compliance with U.S. law, they will not discriminate against participants based on age, race, gender, or national origin.

6. Permit Direct Commercial Flights. We recommend that the OFAC authorize and license direct commercial flights to Cuba. Current regulations authorize daily direct charter flights between Miami and Havana. It is not in the U.S. national interest that non-U.S. carriers capture the entire market of expanding travel to and from Cuba. We therefore recommend that American commercial airlines begin to open routes to Havana and perhaps other Cuban cities not only from Miami but from other major cities and hubs. We recommend also that the United States and Cuba negotiate a civil aviation agreement to this end.

7. Amend Spending Limits. Current regulations limit licensed travelers to Cuba to spending no more than $100 per day, plus transportation and expenses for the acquisition of informational materials, including artwork. We recommend that the OFAC impose this limit only on spending in state-owned enterprises and joint ventures.

8. Expand Diplomatic and Consular Services. The recommendations in this report will greatly increase demands on the U.S. Interests Section in Cuba. Current U.S. consular services in Cuba should not be limited to Havana. We recommend that the United States open a subsection of its Havana consular office in Santiago de Cuba, a step that will also increase our ability to fill the quota of 5,000 slots available for Cuban political refugees

each year. We recommend that the United States negotiate a reciprocal agreement with Cuba that will allow each country to expand its consular services to accommodate increased contact between citizens of both countries.

9. Demand Reciprocity in Limitations on Activities by U.S. and Cuban Diplomats. At present, an imbalance exists wherein American diplomats in Havana are denied access to government offices, the courts, the National Assembly, the University, and virtually all official Cuban facilities other than the Ministry of Foreign Relations. The same is not the case in Washington, where Cuban diplomats freely walk the halls of Congress, meet with elected representatives, speak at universities, and otherwise have access to a fairly wide range of American governmental and nongovernmental representatives. We recommend that the United States and Cuba discuss a reciprocal widening of the areas of permitted activities for diplomats in both countries.

BASKET THREE: HUMANITARIAN AID

The 1992 Cuban Democracy Act established regulations addressing the humanitarian needs of the Cuban population. Since then, the economic crisis has worsened. This basket of recommendations includes humanitarian measures that will help relieve the suffering of the Cuban people today while building the basis for a better relationship between Cuba and the United States in the future.

Humanitarian Aid Recommendations
1. Institute "Cash and Carry" for Foods and Medicines. We applaud the intention behind recent efforts in the Congress and the executive branch to facilitate the increased delivery of humanitarian aid to Cuba. Recognizing that a consensus is emerging to extend humanitarian aid to benefit the Cuban people directly, we recommend that the president accelerate and facilitate this process by eliminating all licensing with respect to donation and sales of food, medicines, and medical products to nongovern-

mental and humanitarian institutions such as hospitals, which are nominally state-run but are not primarily instruments of repression, while authorizing all necessary financial transactions for cash payments on a noncredit basis. We recommend that the State Department issue a specific list of repressive institutions that are to be excluded as potential aid recipients or buyers.[3] To further facilitate donations and sales of food, medicines, and medical products, we recommend that the United States issue licenses to U.S. private voluntary and religious organizations, nongovernmental organizations, and businesses to operate distribution centers in Cuba.

2. Promote People-to-People Aid. We support American engagement with a wide range of civil institutions, particularly those in the private sector; e.g., the emerging church-run medical clinics and humanitarian institutions such as hospitals, which are nominally state-run but are not primarily instruments of repression. With the support and encouragement of the Congress, the administration has significantly widened the opening for Americans to launch humanitarian, people-to-people programs in Cuba. We encourage American local governments and nongovernmental organizations to "adopt" their Cuban counterparts, whether through church, hospital, school, environmental, or university programs. The United States should eliminate the need for licenses for humanitarian donations and shipments, including material aid and cash, and should grant a general license for related travel. We recommend that the United States impose no limit on the amount of material donations under such programs, while requiring a license for cash donations above $10,000 per year by any one American institution to its Cuban counterpart—with the exception of private foundations, for which we recom-

---

[3] For instance, identifying the Ministry of Interior as an excluded institution would have the effect of excluding fire departments throughout the island, which in our view are legitimate potential recipients of aid or purchasers of food and medicine. On the other hand, the Ministry of Interior is also responsible for running the Bureau of Prisons, an agency that international human rights groups regularly charge with engaging in repressive activities. Thus, in carrying out this recommendation, the State Department should focus sanctions as specifically as possible on those agencies that are actually responsible for repressive activities.

mend waiving that limit and permitting the grant-making bodies to use their own institutional criteria to determine in-country funding limits. In the same spirit as that which underlies the Basket One recommendation regarding family remittances, we recommend the United States permit American families to adopt and send remittances to Cuban families of up to $10,000 per year.

3. Allow Cuban Americans to Claim Relatives as Dependents. Currently American citizens with dependent relatives living in Canada and Mexico can claim them as dependents for federal income tax purposes if they meet the other relevant IRS requirements. We recommend an amendment to U.S. tax laws so that American taxpayers with dependents who are residents of Cuba can also claim this deduction.

4. Provide Benefits for Families of Prisoners of Conscience. Under current law, the president may extend humanitarian assistance to victims of political repression and their families in Cuba. We recommend that the United States encourage our European and Latin American allies to join with us to provide support and assistance to family members who, because of their imprisoned relatives' peaceful political activities, may find themselves denied access to jobs by Cuban authorities or who have lost the wages of an imprisoned spouse or parent. If it is not possible to deliver the funds to affected families in Cuba today, we recommend that the funds be paid into interest-bearing accounts in the United States and elsewhere, free of all tax, to accumulate until such time as the intended recipients can collect.

BASKET FOUR: THE PRIVATE SECTOR

Private-sector, for-profit business activity in Cuba by U.S. individuals and corporations raises a number of difficult issues. To take one example, Cuban labor laws currently require foreign investors to contract Cuban workers indirectly through the Ministry of Labor and Social Security, a violation of internationally recognized labor rights. While there are some minor exceptions to the rule, the over-all result of these requirements is that the foreign investor pays several hundred dollars per month per worker, but the worker receives no more than a few dollars per month. By allowing the Cuban state to control which Cubans have access to coveted jobs with foreign investors, the system reinforces the Cuban regime's control over the lives of the Cuban people.

Until a complete settlement of the claims resulting from nationalization of private property in Cuba is reached, U.S. investors in Cuba could conceivably end up buying or profiting from nationalized property and find their titles or earnings challenged under international law by the original owners. Many trademark and other intellectual property problems involve the two countries. Cuba's insistence that most foreign investment take the form of joint ventures in which the Cuban government often retains a controlling interest is another serious problem, as is the incompatibility of Cuba's legal and financial arrangements with U.S. trade policy.

In formulating our recommendations about private U.S. business in Cuba, we once again try to walk a middle way. These recommendations open a door for Cuba progressively to escape some of the consequences of the embargo—to the extent that the Cuban government gives Cubans the right to own and operate their own enterprises, allows foreign companies to hire Cubans directly, and begins to respect basic internationally recognized labor rights. The recommendations will make clear to the Cuban people (as well as to other countries) that the chief obstacle to Cuba's economic progress is not U.S. policy but the Cuban government's hostility toward private property and independent business, its control of the economy and investment, its persistent appropriation of the lion's share of the wages of working Cubans, and its unwillingness to allow companies to pay fair wages to their employees or permit them to engage in free collective bargaining.

Private Sector Recommendations

1. Begin Licensing Some American Business Activity. We recommend that four limited categories of American businesses receive licenses to operate in Cuba. The first category—already eligible for licensing—can generally be described as newsgathering or the procurement of informational material. The second category relates to supporting licensed travel, including transportation to and from Cuba and services to assist the private sector, such as *paladares* and bed and breakfasts, in capturing the business resulting from increased licensed travel. (Examples of this type of business are guides and Internet registries that provide information for foreign visitors about private restaurants, bed and breakfasts, car services, and other private services available in Cuba.) The third category includes activities related to distribution of humanitarian aid and sales. In the fourth category are businesses that facilitate activities related to culture, including the production of new cultural materials, the purchase and sale of artworks and other cultural materials, and the verification of Cuban adherence to intellectual property rights agreements. These four categories, in our judgment, provide such clear benefits that we recommend the U.S. government begin licensing private businesses to operate in all these fields, each of which involves primarily activities that support objectives clearly specified in U.S. law. The U.S. government should routinely license business operations in Cuba restricted to these four areas and allow the transactions and support services necessary to conduct them.

2. Condition Additional American Business Activity. Beyond these limited areas, a number of groups have looked at how to structure U.S. business relations in Cuba without reinforcing the status quo. One of the best known is a set of guidelines known as the Arcos Principles. Drawing from these and similar efforts such as the Sullivan Principles in South Africa and the MacBride Principles in Northern Ireland, we recommend that American businesses demonstrate that they can satisfy three core conditions before being licensed to invest in Cuba for activities

beyond the four specified above: the ability to hire and pay Cuban workers directly and not through a government agency; a pledge by the company to respect workers' internationally recognized rights of free association; and a pledge by the company not to discriminate against Cuban citizens in the provision of goods and services. (The final condition is designed to counter the practice of "tourism apartheid" in which certain foreign-owned and -operated facilities do not allow Cuban citizens to use their facilities, even when they have the money to pay.) We would also encourage U.S. investors—indeed, all foreign investors in Cuba—to provide reading rooms, classes, Internet access, and other on-site facilities so that their employees can enjoy wider access to the world. If Cuba should change its labor laws to make compliance with these principles easier, it would then become much easier for U.S. companies to invest. For a specific business license to be approved, however, it is enough for a particular company to demonstrate that it can satisfy the three criteria listed above.

If and when Cuban law is changed to facilitate compliance with the core principles outlined above, or if Cuban authorities begin to grant exemptions and waivers on a routine basis, we would recommend that Congress and the executive consider broader application of such licensing. In all cases, licensing a business to operate under these provisions would in no way reduce the risk of incurring Helms-Burton penalties for trafficking in confiscated property.

BASKET FIVE: THE NATIONAL INTEREST

National Interest Recommendations
1. Conduct Military-to-Military Confidence-Building Measures. Both Presidents Bush and Clinton have stated that the United States has no aggressive intentions toward Cuba, and the Pentagon has concluded that Cuba poses no significant national secu-

rity threat to the United States. We believe, therefore, that it is in our national interest to promote greater ties and cooperation with the Cuban military. We believe the more confident the Cuban military is that the United States will not take military advantage of a political or economic opening, the more likely it is that elements of the Cuban Armed Forces will tolerate or support such an opening and the less justifiable it will be to divert public resources from social needs to maintaining a defense force far beyond the legitimate needs of the nation. We believe this process should proceed on a step-by-step basis with many of the initial contacts through civilian agencies, both governmental and nongovernmental. We also believe it would be useful for the United States to encourage an opening of relations between militaries in other nations that have carried out successful transitions from communist regimes to democratic societies, such as those in Eastern Europe and, where appropriate, in Latin America. We also recommend that the Pentagon and State Department initiate conversations with the Cuban Armed Forces and others to reduce tensions, promote mutual confidence-building measures, and lay the basis for the improvement of relations in the future should Cuba move toward a democratic transition.

2. Probe Areas for Counternarcotics Cooperation. Cuba sits at the center of a substantial drug trade in the Caribbean Basin. Its neighbor to the east, Haiti, has recently emerged as a major port for cocaine transit from South America to the United States. Despite the outstanding indictments against some Cuban officials for alleged drug trafficking, the Cuban state has both the geographical and the institutional resources to help America fight the war on drugs if the Cuban regime chooses to do so. In recent years, the United States and Cuba have cooperated on a limited case-by-case basis in counternarcotics efforts in the Caribbean Basin. We recommend that the appropriate U.S. government agencies test Cuba's willingness to take serious steps to demonstrate its good faith in furthering cooperation in the counternarcotics arena, while protecting the confidentiality of

U.S. intelligence sources and methods. We note that Cuba still harbors individuals indicted in the United States on serious drug trafficking charges. Clearly, limited cooperation in this area will depend on a demonstrated willingness by the Cuban government to address this issue seriously.

3. Institute Routine Executive Branch Consultations with Congress and Others on Cuba Policy. We recommend continued and enhanced bipartisan consultations by the executive branch with Congress and with a broad range of leaders representing political, social, and economic groups in the Cuban American, humanitarian, religious, academic, and cultural communities. As we have seen in U.S. policy toward Central America, and throughout most of the post–Cold War era, a bipartisan consensus between Congress and the executive is a precondition for sustaining a long-term, successful U.S. foreign policy initiative.

4. Form a Working Group on the 21st Century. When people in both the United States and Cuba talk about the future relationship between the two countries, they often speak of the "normalization of relations." In fact, the United States and Cuba have not had "normal" relations since the United States intervened to end Spanish rule in 1898. Since the current Cuban regime came to power in 1959, it has employed a formidable propaganda machine to cloak Cuban nationalism in a banner of anti-American rhetoric. Cuban schoolchildren are taught to view the Cuban revolution as the only legitimate guarantor of national sovereignty and to regard the United States as a constant threat to Cuba's independence. However opposed the United States has been and remains to the present Cuban government, the American people have no interest in intruding upon Cuba's sovereignty, independence, or national identity. As Cuba inaugurates its second century of independence, we recommend that the Council on Foreign Relations or another similar private institution convene a binational working group of scholars, policy analysts, and others to begin working out an agenda for a new relationship between the United States and Cuba in the 21st century, ana-

lyzing a range of complex bilateral and regional issues, including the resolution of outstanding property claims; the status of the U.S. military base at Guantánamo Bay; the implications for the Western Hemisphere of the restoration of a Cuban sugar quota; the impact on the Caribbean economy of resuming normal bilateral trade relations; Cuban participation in the Caribbean Basin Initiative (CBI) and the Free Trade Area of the Americas (FTAA); prospects for Cuba's reentry into the Organization of American States (OAS); and the integration of Cuba into the international financial system.

FOLLOW-UP STEPS

These proposals represent a beginning of what we hope will become a growing bipartisan policy toward Cuba. We believe that responsible officials and interested individuals and groups should monitor the effect of these recommendations, should they be implemented, and after a reasonable period of time assess whether changes, modifications, and additional steps are warranted.

ADDITIONAL AND DISSENTING VIEWS

On Expanded Telecommunications with Cuba

The Cuban Democracy Act properly sought to expand opportunities for communications between Americans and Cubans. Our recommendations note the need to follow through on the Cuban Democracy Act's call for direct postal service between the two countries. We would go further, however, and reexamine the Cuban Democracy Act provisions regarding telecommunications between Cuba and the United States. It seems to us that telecommunications and computer technology have evolved rapidly enough, even in the relatively few years since the enactment of the Cuban Democracy Act and Helms-Burton, to merit such a reexamination. Among other things, we believe the OFAC should consider licensing U.S. companies and firms to provide communications facilities and services on the island, as long as those facilities do not and could not reasonably be expected to enhance the military posture of the regime or otherwise facilitate actions inimical to U.S. interests. (Today, U.S. telecommunication companies are limited to running wires up to Cuba's shores and must, therefore, interconnect with the decrepit Cuban telephone system.) In the meantime, the Cuban telecommunications system—including access to the Internet—will eventually be the mechanism by which information is disseminated. As such, it is a fundamental element of many of the recommendations we have made and should be strengthened and improved. We see no reason why U.S. technology and know-how should be excluded from the process of upgrading Cuba's telecommunications infrastructure.

Allen R. Adler
Mario L. Baeza
Philip Peters

The Case Against the Necessity of Executive and Congressional Consensus

When a number of us first approached this project, we decided to use as our point of departure the most recent congressional and executive branch consensus regarding Cuba policy—namely, the Cuban Liberty and Democratic Solidarity Act of 1996, commonly referred to as the Helms-Burton Act, and the Cuban Democracy Act of 1992 (collectively, the "Acts"). Instead of focusing on the punitive measures contained in the Acts, however, we turned our attention to those provisions that call for increased contacts between Cubans and U.S. citizens, and to other measures designed to encourage and support the growth of private enterprise and individual freedoms in Cuba. In particular, we focused on the plain meaning and intent of the Acts, which, among other things, are designed to "assist the Cuban people in regaining their freedom and prosperity," as well as to "seek a peaceful transition to democracy and resumption of economic growth in Cuba." Starting from this presupposition, we concluded that a much wider range of permissible activity and contacts between U.S. and Cuban citizens are justified under the Acts than those currently permitted by administrative orders. We then set out to come up with policy prescriptions that, in our view, were vital or desirable in accomplishing certain goals.

I believe the Task Force Report accomplishes this objective. However, I would go further and make clear that, as a legal matter, the implementation of most of our recommendations does not require both congressional and executive branch consensus. I believe that substantially all of our recommendations can, as a legal matter, be implemented by executive orders or administrative actions only.

While I concur that as a matter of political pragmatism it would be desirable, if not essential, for the executive and legislative branches to proceed hand-in-hand, I do not wish to concede that the presidential powers to implement the law do not extend to the taking of actions recommended in the Task Force Report, except with respect to certain private-sector initiatives which would, in fact, require amendments to the existing law.

Mario L. Baeza

On the Benefits for the United States from Increased Contact
The report of the Independent Task Force is focused almost entirely on what Cubans can gain from additional U.S. contacts. I would like to make explicit what is perhaps implicit in our report—namely, that there are many benefits we Americans can derive from increased contact with the Cuban people. The U.S. business community has a keen interest in making its own assessments of who is who in Cuba and of the nature of the problems, risks, and opportunities that it is likely to encounter in a post-regime era. In the fields of health care, medicine, bioengineering, and computer science, there are advances by Cuban scientists and professionals that we could benefit from. Similarly, there is much to Cuban cultural life, including the celebration of the Afro-Cuban culture, that, even today, can enrich us greatly.

Mario L. Baeza

On the Cuban Economy and the Scope of Proposed Changes in U.S. Travel and Investment Policy
We signed the report but want to express our own assessment of U.S. policy and the situation in Cuba, and our consequent belief

that U.S. interests would be served by more far-reaching changes in policy.

Whatever its successes in the past, American policy toward Cuba today is counterproductive at its core. The 1960s-vintage objective of the political and economic isolation of Cuba made sense when the Soviet Union still existed and Cuba's behavior threatened security and democratic development in the Americas. Today, those factors are gone and the policy chiefly serves to limit American influence by blocking the flow of people, commerce, and ideas. Moreover, it restricts freedoms of American citizens in ways that have no justification in the absence of a security threat.

The policy sends a deeply hostile message to the Cuban people. U.S. law bars trade, even in benign goods. It bars U.S. investment and uses extraordinary legal means to discourage foreign investment. It calls for the United Nations to impose a global trade embargo on Cuba. It bans any ship that calls on Cuba from entering American ports for six months, even if that ship delivered only rice and aspirin to Cuba.

It is little wonder that Cuba's Catholic bishops call this a "cruel" policy that attempts to "destabilize the government by using hunger and want to pressure civic society to revolt." One is hard pressed to find dissidents or Cubans on the street who see virtue or political reason in this approach.

In sum, American policy toward Cuba lacks the magnanimity and confidence that befit a great power whose chief global adversary has vanished.

The report mentions small businesses, but does not capture the full extent of economic change in Cuba. A series of limited openings—incentive-based agriculture, farmers' markets, small business, foreign investment—have, in addition to other measures such as the legalization of foreign currency, created a new economic sector governed by market mechanisms, not state planning. Workers who earn tips or high dollar wages from foreign investors generate demand for produce at farmers' markets or for small business services. Family remittances add to this demand.

This sector would surely expand if Cuban policies were more open, but even now it represents a significant step forward for Cuban and American interests. It has raised Cubans' incomes and skill levels, and has introduced new ways of doing business that prepare Cuba for a more capitalist future.

We are confident that greater contact between Americans and Cubans will benefit U.S. interests, and we offer some illustrative recommendations below.

Today's severe restrictions on American citizens' travel to Cuba have no national security justification, no political logic in the Cuban context, and no precedent in U.S. policy toward the Soviet Union or China since the 1970s. Our colleagues constructively support "targeted" travel, but we go further. All American citizens personify American ideas and values. The travel ban and its onerous licensing processes should be dropped. Americans traveling freely, without government licensing or program restrictions, will support the expansion of free-market activity in Cuba and will build links with Cuban society that no government program would envision.

Under the Helms-Burton law, American policy allows sanctions to be eased only when Cuba's leadership and political system are replaced. Previous law allowed sanctions to be eased in a calibrated response to positive reforms undertaken in Cuba. This provision should be restored.

Regarding investment in Cuba, we agree that changes in Cuban policy are desirable, but we also recognize that foreign investors working under current Cuban law are improving the lot of Cuban workers today. We therefore urge a bolder step: permitting full economic relations in a single sector such as agriculture, telecommunications, or housing. As commerce develops, American companies will surely bring benefits to Cuban workers and their families, and they could encourage positive change in Cuban policy. Further action could depend on the results of this single-sector experiment.

Ted Galen Carpenter
Craig Fuller
Franklin W. Knight
Philip Peters

The Case for Ending Discrimination Against Cuban Scholars and Artists
While the Task Force Report indicates that, because of pressure from Cuban authorities, U.S. institutions have barred Cuban Americans from participating in existing exchange programs and states that such practices should not continue, it makes no mention of continuing efforts by some groups to prevent Cuban scholars and artists from participating in scholarly and cultural events in the United States. Both types of discrimination and censorship should cease.

Rodolfo O. de la Garza

The Case for Maintaining the Embargo
This report correctly emphasizes the importance of strengthening civil society in Cuba to help bring about a peaceful transition to democracy on the island. Efforts toward this end will be undermined, however, if most of the new resources reaching Cuba end up in government, rather than in private, hands. This is why the embargo must remain in place for now. If democracy is to develop in Cuba, the balance of power and resources between the state

and the civil society that currently exists on the island must be reversed so as to favor the people.

Mark Falcoff
Daniel W. Fisk
Susan Kaufman Purcell

The Case for Executive-Congressional Agreement
Since the Cuban Democracy Act of 1992, and as reiterated in the Cuban Liberty and Democratic Solidarity Act of 1996, U.S. policy toward Cuba is based on an embargo on the Castro regime and efforts to support the emergence of a civil society in Cuba. This Task Force Report, for the most part, affirms and builds on this framework and avoids the premise that U.S. policy must change for Castro to change. In fact, the strength of this report is its attempt to find ways to build civil society despite the continuing intransigence of Castro. For these reasons, I endorse the general policy thrust of the report. One aspect of the report which raises a concern, however, is that many of the recommendations call for unilateral executive implementation even while the Task Force notes the importance of a bipartisan consensus to a policy's effectiveness. This seems to contradict the Task Force's call for enhanced executive-congressional consultations. Many of the report's recommendations have merit, but part of building a bipartisan consensus is executive-congressional agreement on moving forward, not unilateral presidential actions. These recommendations will be effective only if such consultations would occur before implementation or changes in policy. Executive-congressional agreement on these recommendations will signal that U.S. resolve on behalf of a democratic Cuba, not rapprochement with the Castro regime, remains firm and consistent.

Daniel W. Fisk

The Case Against Counternarcotics Cooperation

The report's recommendation regarding counternarcotics cooperation is misguided on two levels. First, as such distinguished Americans as Milton Friedman and George Shultz have pointed out, Washington's hemispheric war on drugs is a futile policy that causes serious collateral social and economic damage to numerous countries. Second, cooperation on narcotics issues would require U.S. collaboration with the most odious and repressive agencies in Cuba's police-state bureaucracy. Such collaboration would send precisely the wrong message to Cubans who want to weaken these instruments of repression.

Ted Galen Carpenter

The Case Against Further Counternarcotics Cooperation

Any initiatives for cooperation should clearly place the burden on Cuba to show that it respects international standards in combating illegal drugs. Specifically, by harboring fugitives—including Cuban officials facing outstanding indictments for drug trafficking—Cuba has shown little, if any, serious interest in combating this threat to the hemisphere. Even more problematic, however, is that any expansion beyond the current case-by-case cooperation would require U.S. law enforcement to engage directly with Castro's state security apparatus. If we require human rights to be respected by other entities with whom we engage in counternarcotics efforts, the same threshold is doubly important in the case of Cuba. At most, the Task Force should recommend a comprehensive U.S. government assessment of the extent of drug trafficking in and through Cuba, including an assessment of any official Cuban complicity, a briefing prepared for the Congress, and a determination by the two political branches as to the appropriate next steps.

Mark Falcoff
Daniel W. Fisk

On Potential Problems with Facilitating "Targeted Travel"
There is a qualitative difference between those seeking to help, or reunite with, their families and those simply seeking something "forbidden." Recommending a "general license" for tourist agencies potentially facilitates tourism for those who have no demonstrable professional or other serious interest in Cuba, but who are interested in the novelty of leisure tourism, or who are investors scavenging to make a quick buck or to exploit a controlled labor force. These serve the interests of neither the United States nor the Cuban people. Such a result would benefit a sector of the Cuban economy that is a significant source of hard currency for the regime.

Daniel W. Fisk

The Case for Executive-Congressional Agreement on Sales of Food
Given that the extent of the president's authority to authorize sales of food unilaterally is uncertain, I must dissent from the recommendation that the president change the current structure by unilateral action. While I support developing ways to provide food assistance, any change should be a decision by both political branches of government.

Daniel W. Fisk

On the Complexity of Food and Medicine Sales to Cuba
U.S. law currently allows the sale of medicines and medical supplies to Cuba. It is doubtful that the Cuban government is interested in this, having made only one effort to purchase anything, despite repeated positive efforts by U.S. officials and private citizens to facilitate the provision of supplies the Cuban government claims it cannot get from anywhere else but the United States. More significantly, regarding the food situation, the fact that an island that was an exporter of food prior to Castro's ascendance cannot feed itself after nearly 40 years of the Castro regime is a consequence of that system's failure, not the U.S. embargo. The United States remains the most generous nation in assisting the victims of natural or man-made disasters; Cuba is clearly the latter. On the other hand, there is a purpose for daring the regime to live up to its rhetorical commitment to provide for the Cuban people: every dollar spent on food and medicine is one less dollar spent directly on the repressive apparatus of the state. There should be no illusions about Castro's interest in food and medicine, but there should be no mistake about our humanitarian objectives to mitigate the odious consequences for the people resulting from that regime. Pursuing our humanitarian objectives while minimizing benefits to the Castro regime is a delicate process that requires a positive consulting process between the executive and legislative branches.

Daniel W. Fisk

The Case Against Expanded Military-to-Military Contacts
The United States has made clear that it has no aggressive intentions toward Cuba, and the U.S. military has conducted itself accordingly, even when Cuban aircraft have violated U.S. airspace or shot down civilian aircraft over international waters. Cuban military tolerance of democratic change is dependent on the Cuban leadership, not the United States. The United States also has enunciated

its willingness to assist the Cuban military in a democratic transition. At most, we should be encouraging the governments and militaries of the former communist regimes in Eastern Europe to engage their military counterparts in Cuba. To have the U.S. military engage in such measures with a country that remains on the U.S. State Department list of countries supporting terrorism, beyond the monthly meeting related to Guantánamo, would legitimize an instrument of Castro's repression.

Daniel W. Fisk

The Case Against Access to the United States by High-Level Cuban Officials

In our view, the degree of access afforded to Cuban government officials in "Basket Two: The Open Door" is excessive. Cuban cabinet ministers and high-ranking parliamentarians are complicit in the regime's repression and should be denied access to the United States.

Daniel W. Fisk
Adrian Karatnycky

The Case Against Official Exchanges

We support most of the humanitarian recommendations, but the report goes too far. The premise of the exercise was supposed to be to bypass the regime and start the rebuilding of Cuban civil society. Yet, the report urges exchanges with the most senior government and military officials on the odd theory that they will be agents of change. In Central Europe, on the contrary, the most successful new democracies are those that went furthest with lustration—that is, purging the senior levels of their institutions (civil service, military, universities, etc.) of communist hacks. Similarly, a "Working Group on the 21st Century" with such regime-approved individuals strikes us as quite naïve.

Moreover, the report is wrong to imply that its recommendations will promote political change. The regime is not in its Gorbachev phase, but at its most Stalinist—witness the recent crushing of the Concilio Cubano. This is another reason to avoid legitimizing the regime, and to stick to modest measures that may ease the burden of ordinary Cubans and help restore private institutions.

The regime is doomed anyway, no matter what we do, so U.S. policy has considerable margin for error. But we need not be so eager to use it all up.

Daniel W. Fisk
Peter W. Rodman

DISSENTING VIEWS SUBMITTED BY OBSERVERS

The Case for a Fundamental Reassessment of Cuba Policy
While I understand and sympathize with the desire for consensus and bipartisanship and have the highest regard for participants in the Task Force, I regret that the report is not more forceful and ambitious. I also regret that the report does not explicitly support the idea put forward by Secretary Lawrence Eagleburger and other distinguished foreign policy practitioners for a bipartisan national commission on Cuba. Cuba policy deserves fundamental reassessment, not tinkering at the edges. Above all, the debate needs to be lifted out of the straightjacket of narrow electoral political considerations where it is currently mired. A broad-based bipartisan national commission may or may not recommend drastic changes such as the ending of the embargo, but it is essential in my view that an open debate take place on the fundamental questions and the sooner the better.

I personally do not agree with the premise that the embargo has been a success. I have always believed that openness is the best policy, and that contact, not ostracism, is a greater threat to dictatorships, be they of the left or the right. This is especially true where regimes like Castro's can exploit a strong history of nationalism. In the Cuban case, it is an inescapable fact that despite 40 years of embargo Castro remains in power; he has not fallen. He may indeed be "contained" in politico-military terms, but it is also a fact of life that Havana is awash with Europeans and Canadians, that the papal visit will be followed this year by the Ibero-American summit and a parade of Latin American and European leaders, and that there are very few U.S. luminaries who can resist the chance to sup with Castro if invited. Nor for that matter did the embargo restrain Castro's adventures in Africa and Latin America in the past. It would be nice to think that small unilateral steps will undermine the regime and promote fundamental political change in Cuba, but I do not believe that they will. They are too dependent on Castro's implicit agreement. Castro has never carried through on positive overtures of this type from Washington in the past, preferring to kick away the ladder when it seemed a mini détente might be in the offing. I am even more skeptical of the proposition that one can play favorites with functionaries within his apparatus of power; if anything it will expose them to risk and discovery. Castro has never hesitated to remove potential threats to his power, even when it involved the judicial murder of the most popular leader of his Angolan expeditionary force, General Ochoa.

Yet one thing does seem certain: it is that change, when it happens, will come quickly and unexpectedly, and that once Castro is gone his ramshackle regime will collapse in short order. Like Louis XIV, even Castro seems to believe that "après moi le déluge." It is therefore critical that the United States free itself from the legal and emotional handicaps that now bedevil its Cuba policy and that will prevent the U.S. government and U.S. society, including Cuban Americans, from reacting with speed, flexibility, and good sense when the happy moment of liberation arrives. To promote minor modification in the status quo is no answer. It leaves Castro with a situation he has long known how to navigate and exploit. And it leaves the United States with a policy that perpetuates the all-too-familiar pattern of paternalism and micromanagement toward Cuba's internal affairs that has bedeviled U.S.-Cuban relations now for over a century.

Kenneth R. Maxwell

On the General Limitations of the Report
The Task Force should be congratulated for the spirit in which they undertook this enterprise, and for their effort to find some consensus on initiatives that can be taken within the framework of the current U.S. policy of isolating the Castro regime.

The report's specific policy recommendations are a mixed bag—some have merit, others go too far, and still others are too timid. But the basic framework is correct: the U.S. embargo has indeed been a success, as the report definitively states, and the Congress and the executive branch should now work together in developing bold new measures to support democratic change in Cuba and to help the Cuban people build a civil society independent of the communist regime.

The major problem with the report is that, for the most part, it does not require any real systematic changes in Cuba as a condition for changes in U.S. policy. The Task Force Report correctly cites Poland as a model for promoting democratic change in Cuba, and notes that each change in U.S. sanctions on communist Poland in the 1980s was made as a quid pro quo for some form of systematic change in Poland—the release of political prisoners, legalization of the Solidarity Party, etc.

Unfortunately, there is no discussion in the report of similarly conditioning many recommended changes in U.S. policy toward Cuba on release of political prisoners, legalization of opposition parties, legalization of independent press, etc. Only once does the report lay out such a quid pro quo, when it suggests that broad U.S.

investment in Cuba be permitted only when Cuba changes its labor laws to permit direct hiring of workers, free association of labor, and other freedoms laid out in the Arcos Principles. Similar requirements for change in Cuba should have been included as conditions for some of the Task Force's other recommendations.

Of course, Castro is not likely to engage in such a give-and-take with the United States—but his successors might. The Task Force missed an excellent opportunity to recommend ways these future leaders could trade a normalization of relations with the United States for Cuba's democratic transition.

Indeed, the Task Force would better have broken its recommendations into two distinct categories: steps that could be taken immediately to break the information blockade and to increase the flow of humanitarian aid and support for civil society in Cuba, and steps that could be taken in exchange for systematic change in Cuba.

Some recommendations, such as proposed military-to-military contact, are very bad ideas. The motivation is correct: there is a need to communicate to junior officers in the Cuban military that there is life after Castro, and that if they do the right thing during a transition (i.e., don't fire on the people) they will have a place of pride in a democratic Cuba. But the Cuban government will never let U.S. officers have contact with those in the Cuban military who might be open to such a message—only die-hard loyalists will be allowed near the American military. The net effect would be a legitimization of Cuba's instruments of repression, without the effect of increased communication with the desired elements in the Cuban military—thus violating the Task Force's own principle that "no change in U.S. policy should have the primary effect of consolidating or legitimizing the status quo on the island." We must find other ways to communicate with these officers that do not legitimize the Cuban regime.

The same goes for recommendations for government-to-government cooperation on issues such as the environment and drugs. Today, some 90 fugitives wanted on criminal charges in the United States—including several Cuban officials indicted in U.S. courts on drug-smuggling charges—are being given refuge in Cuba by the Castro regime. At a bare minimum, Cuba should be required to extradite these fugitives before any drug cooperation is even contemplated. The Task Force does not make clear what benefits, if any, would be achieved that outweigh the legitimization such contacts would provide the Cuban regime.

On the positive side, some of the recommendations to help strengthen indigenous private enterprise on the island are worthy of consideration. Thanks to combined pressure from the U.S. embargo and the loss of Soviet subsidies, Castro has been forced to allow some private businesses to function on the island (principally *paladares*, small private restaurants where Cubans can serve food in their homes and employ immediate family members). However small, these cracks in the wall of Cuban communism must be exploited. Helping existing and potential private entrepreneurs expand space in Cuba independent of communist society is a worthy goal.

The recommendation to allow all Americans, and not just Cuban Americans, to send remittances to Cuba is also worthy of consideration. This would allow a church in New Jersey to adopt a church in Santiago de Cuba by sending donations that will help the Cuban church expand its space in society through programs for the elderly, running private pharmacies and health clinics, or other private activities that help build an independent civil society in Cuba.

However, the recommendation to raise the remittance limit to $10,000 (up from the current $1,200 per person) would essentially blow a hole in the embargo, allowing back-channel private investment on the island and large cash flows into the coffers of the regime. The administration's recent decision to maintain the $1,200 limit but allow all Americans to send remittances is a more prudent course of action.

The report's recommendations on "targeted travel" are also much too loosely structured. Granting special multiple-entry licenses to travel agencies, which could then invite clients to travel under these licenses, would amount to a lifting of the tourism travel ban. Narrower measures to facilitate increased contacts with Americans traveling to aid the development of Cuban civil society would be preferable.

The "cash and carry" recommendations on the sale and donation of food and medicines also go too far. The goal of increased donations and distribution of humanitarian relief is indeed desirable, because it helps private Cuban relief agencies to expand their space in society and decreases the Cuban people's dependence on the state. But sales to the Cuban government are another matter. Any sale of food would require an act of Congress. The sale of medicine and medical equipment is already allowed under U.S. law, yet Cuba does not buy American medical products—because it cannot afford to. Better that the United States simply give them food and medicine, and legislation has been introduced in the Senate to facilitate humanitarian donations and give $100 million in free food and medicine to Cuba via private Cuban nongovernmental organizations.

In the end, some of the Task Force's recommendations will prove unworkable, while others might be worth considering if conditioned on specific changes in Cuba. But the broad thrust of the report is correct: taking the embargo off the table, bipartisan consensus can be developed on new ways to reach out to the Cuban people, expand civil society on the island, and break Castro's embargo on his own people. Some of these ideas could become the basis for further discussion between Congress and the administration on developing bipartisan Cuba legislation.

Marc A. Thiessen

TASK FORCE MEMBERS

ALLEN R. ADLER*, currently a private investor, is involved in a broad range of nonprofit activities. Among others, he is a trustee of the Simon Wiesenthal Center and serves on the board of the World Policy Institute. In his earlier career, he was an executive with Columbia Pictures Industries and Paribas North America. He is a graduate of Princeton University's Woodrow Wilson School of Public and International Affairs and the Harvard Business School.

BERNARD W. ARONSON served as Assistant Secretary of State for Inter-American Affairs from June 1989 through July 1993, under two U.S. presidents, longer then any other holder of that position. Prior to leaving his post, Mr. Aronson was awarded the State Department's highest civilian honor, the Distinguished Service Award, by then Secretary of State Warren Christopher. Mr. Aronson served as International Adviser to Goldman Sachs & Co. after leaving the State Department, and currently serves as Chairman of ACON Investments L.L.C., which manages Newbridge Andean Partners L.P., a private equity fund that makes direct investments in Latin American companies, primarily in the Andean bloc of South America.

MARIO L. BAEZA* is Chairman and Chief Executive Officer of TCW/Latin America Partners, L.L.C., and various related entities. He is the former President of Wasserstein Parella International, Ltd., and a former partner in the international law firm of Debevoise & Plimpton. Mr. Baeza is a member of the Board of Directors of the Council on Foreign Relations, and several other for-profit and nonprofit institutions.

JEFFREY L. BEWKES is Chairman and Chief Executive Officer of Home Box Office. He is responsible for the overall management of the world's largest premium television company, which operates multiple premium networks in the United States, Europe, Asia, and Latin America, as well as HBO's many other lines of business.

TED GALEN CARPENTER*† is Vice President for Defense and Foreign Policy Studies at the Cato Institute in Washington, D.C. He has published numerous texts on security and international affairs.

RODOLFO O. DE LA GARZA*, Vice President of the Tomás Rivera Policy Institute and Mike Hogg Professor of Community Affairs at the University of Texas, is a specialist in ethnic politics. His most recent work, *Family Ties and Ethnic Lobbies*, analyzes how Latino relations with their countries of origin affect U.S. foreign policy.

MARK FALCOFF*† is a resident scholar at the American Enterprise Institute for Public Policy Research in Washington, D.C. He has taught at the universities of Illinois, Oregon, and California (Los Angeles), and at the U.S. Foreign Service Institute. In the 99th Congress he served on the staff of the U.S. Senate Foreign Relations Committee.

DANIEL W. FISK*†, as a senior staff member and Associate Counsel of the Senate Foreign Relations Committee, played a principal staff role in the Cuban Liberty and Democratic Solidarity (LIBERTAD) Act of 1996. He is now an Adjunct Fellow with the Center for Strategic and International Studies, Washington, D.C., a member of the Board of Directors of the Institute for U.S.-Cuba Relations, and a Teaching Associate/Ph.D. candidate in the Department of Political Science at Arizona State University.

CRAIG FULLER*, Chairman of Global Board Services of Korn/Ferry International, is responsible for conducting board and senior-level-executive search assignments in the firm's General Practice. Mr. Fuller served for eight years in the White House as Chief of Staff

---

Note: Institutional affiliations are for identification purposes only.
*Individual largely concurs with the report, but has submitted (an) additional view(s).
†Individual largely concurs with the report, but has submitted (a) dissenting view(s).

to Vice President Bush and as Assistant to President Reagan for Cabinet Affairs. President-elect Bush named Mr. Fuller the Co-director of his presidential transition team.

PETER HAKIM is President of the Inter-American Dialogue, the leading U.S. center for policy analysis and exchange on Western Hemisphere affairs. The author of a regular column for the *Christian Science Monitor*, Mr. Hakim speaks and publishes widely on U.S.–Latin American relations. He serves on boards and advisory committees for the World Bank, Inter-American Development Bank, International Center for Research on Women, Carnegie Endowment for International Peace, and Human Rights Watch/Americas.

GARY C. HUFBAUER is Reginald Jones Senior Fellow at the Institute for International Economics. Previously he was Maurice R. Greenberg Chair and Director of Studies at the Council on Foreign Relations. He is a co-author of *Economic Sanctions Reconsidered.*

ADRIAN KARATNYCKY† is President of Freedom House, a nonpartisan, nonprofit organization that promotes democracy, civil society, and the rule of law, and monitors democratic change, political rights, and civil liberties throughout the world. Mr. Karatnycky is Editor and Director of *Freedom in the World: The Annual Survey of Political Rights and Civil Liberties*. Mr. Karatnycky has been President of Freedom House since September 1993.

M. FAROOQ KATHWARI is Chairman, President, and Chief Executive Officer of Ethan Allen, Inc. He has been President of the company since 1985 and Chairman and Chief Executive Officer since 1988. He is the founder of the Kashmir Study Group and serves on the boards of the Institute for Diplomacy, Georgetown University; the National Retail Federation; and the American Furniture Manufacturers Association.

FRANKLIN W. KNIGHT* is Leonard and Helen R. Stulman Professor of History at the Johns Hopkins University in Baltimore, and

President of the Latin American Studies Association. He has published widely on Cuba, the Caribbean, and Latin America.

PHILIP PETERS* is Senior Fellow at the Alexis de Tocqueville Institution. He formerly served in the State Department's Bureau of Inter-American Affairs during the Reagan and Bush administrations.

SUSAN KAUFMAN PURCELL* is Vice President of the Americas Society and the Council of the Americas in New York. Between 1981 and 1988 she was Senior Fellow and Director of the Latin America Project at the Council on Foreign Relations. She was also a member of the U.S. Department of State's Policy Planning Staff, with responsibility for Latin America and the Caribbean, between 1980 and 1981.

PETER W. RODMAN[†] is Director of National Security Programs at the Nixon Center. He has served as Deputy Assistant to the President for National Security Affairs and as Director of the State Department Policy Planning Staff.

RIORDAN ROETT is Sarita and Don Johnston Professor and Director of the Western Hemisphere Program at the Johns Hopkins Nitze School of Advanced International Studies in Washington, D.C.

WILLIAM D. ROGERS, Senior Partner at Arnold & Porter, Washington, D.C., was formerly Assistant Secretary of State for Inter-American Affairs and Under Secretary of State for International Economic Affairs. In addition, he served on the Law Faculty of Cambridge University and he has served as a member of the Board of Directors at the Council on Foreign Relations.

Note: Institutional affiliations are for identification purposes only.
*Individual largely concurs with the report, but has submitted (an) additional view(s).
[†]Individual largely concurs with the report, but has submitted (a) dissenting view(s).

ALEXANDER F. WATSON was a career Foreign Service Officer for over 30 years, serving chiefly in Latin America, before joining the Nature Conservancy in 1996, where he serves as Vice President and Executive Director for International Conservation. His last three Foreign Service posts were Ambassador to Peru, Deputy Permanent Representative to the United Nations, and Assistant Secretary of State for Inter-American Affairs.

TASK FORCE OBSERVERS

FULTON ARMSTRONG, Director of Inter-American Affairs, National Security Council

JAMES F. DOBBINS, Special Assistant to the President and Senior Director for Inter-American Affairs, National Security Council

KENNETH R. MAXWELL, Nelson and David Rockefeller Senior Fellow for Inter-American Studies and Director, Latin America Program, Council on Foreign Relations

THEODORE E. MCCARRICK, Archdiocese of Newark

BRETT O'BRIEN, Foreign and Defense Policy Adviser, Office of the House Minority Leader

JANICE O'CONNELL, Professional Staff Member, Office of Senator Christopher Dodd

GARDNER G. PECKHAM, Assistant to the Speaker, Office of the Speaker of the House

MARC A. THIESSEN, Press Spokesman, U.S. Senate Committee on Foreign Relations

---

Note: Institutional affiliations are for identification purposes only.

APPENDIXES

STATEMENT ON CUBA BY PRESIDENT WILLIAM J. CLINTON

RELEASED BY THE WHITE HOUSE OFFICE OF THE PRESS SECRETARY

January 5, 1999

Last March, in the wake of Pope John Paul's historic visit to Cuba, I authorized measures designed to ease the plight of the Cuban people and help them prepare for a democratic future. The restoration of direct passenger flights, resumption of family remittances, expansion of people-to-people contacts, and increases in the sale of medicines since then have had a positive impact. They demonstrate the United States' compassion for the Cuban people, our strong interest in building bonds between the citizens of our nations, and our determination to provide the people of Cuba with hope in their struggle against a system that for four decades has denied them even basic human rights.

Building on the success of the measures I announced last March, I am today authorizing additional steps to reach out to the Cuban people:

—Expansion of remittances by allowing any U.S. resident (not only those with families in Cuba) to send limited funds to individual Cuban families as well as to organizations independent of the government.

—Expansion of people-to-people contact through two-way exchanges among academics, athletes, scientists, and others, including streamlining the approval process for such visits.

—Authorization of the sale of food and agricultural inputs to independent non-governmental entities, including religious groups and Cuba's emerging private sector, such as family restaurants and private farmers.

—Authorization of charter passenger flights to cities in Cuba other than Havana and from some cities in the United States other than

Miami in order to facilitate family reunification for persons living outside those cities.

—An effort to establish direct mail service to Cuba, as provided for in the Cuban Democracy Act of 1992.

At the same time, we are taking steps to increase the flow of information to the Cuban people and others around the world, by strengthening Radio and TV Martí and launching new public diplomacy programs in Latin America and Europe to keep international attention focused on the need for change in Cuba. The United States will continue to urge the international community to do more to promote respect for human rights and democratic transition in Cuba.

I am also pleased to announce that I intend to nominate Mr. José "Pepe" Collado and Ms. Avis Lavelle as members of the Advisory Board for Cuba Broadcasting. I further intend to designate Mr. Collado as chairman upon confirmation by the Senate. This important advisory body has been without a chairman since the death of Jorge Mas Canosa more than a year ago. We are processing other nominations and, in cooperation with congressional leaders, will continue to name members of this bipartisan board.

These steps are designed to help the Cuban people without strengthening the Cuban government. They are consistent with our policy of keeping pressure on the regime for democratic change—through the embargo and vigorous diplomatic initiatives—while finding ways to reach out to the Cuban people through humanitarian efforts and help in developing civil society. They are also consistent with the Cuban Democracy Act and the Cuban Liberty and Democratic Solidarity Act. They reflect a strong and growing bipartisan consensus that the United States can and should do more to work with the Cuban people toward a future of democracy and prosperity.

STATEMENT ON CUBA BY SECRETARY OF STATE MADELEINE K. ALBRIGHT

RELEASED BY THE OFFICE OF THE SPOKESMAN,
U.S. DEPARTMENT OF STATE

January 5, 1999

Good afternoon. Last March, in response to Pope John Paul II's inspired pilgrimage to Cuba, the Clinton Administration took steps to reach out to the people of that country to make clear our concern for them and to help make their lives more tolerable.

Today, after consultations with concerned non-governmental organizations and leading members of Congress, we're announcing additional steps in furtherance of that policy. Our goal is to encourage the development in Cuba of peaceful, civic activities that are independent of the government, and that will help the Cuban people prepare for the day when their country is once again free.

First, we will seek to expose additional elements of Cuban society to democratic practices and values by encouraging additional religious, scientific, educational, athletic and other exchanges between our two peoples. We will do this by streamlining visa and licensing procedures for travel between Cuba and the United States by qualified persons other than senior Cuban government officials.

Second, we will expand direct licensed passenger flights to Cuba by authorizing flights from cities other than Miami and to destinations in Cuba other than Havana.

Third, we are broadening the categories of eligible recipients in Cuba for the receipt of financial remittances from the United States. Under this policy, all U.S. residents will be authorized to send up to $300 each quarter to any Cuban family, except for senior government and party leaders. In addition, U.S. citizens and non-governmental organizations will be licensed on a case-by-case basis to send larger remittances to entities in Cuba that are independent of the Cuban government.

Fourth, we will authorize the sale of food and agricultural inputs to private entities and farmers in Cuba. This will also be done on a case-by-case basis and for the purpose of promoting economic activity that is independent of the Cuban government.

Finally, we will seek to restore direct mail service between the United States and Cuba.

These steps are neither designed nor expected to alter our relations with the Cuban government. But taken together, they constitute a major advance in our effort to reach out to the Cuban people. They should help all Cubans to understand that the United States is on their side in the search for economic choice and prosperity, in the quest for the freedom of religion, expression and thought, and in the desire to fulfill José Martí's dream of a Cuba where all may participate freely in the political life of their country.

One year ago, Pope John Paul II brought to Cuba a message of hope and justice, liberty and love. Thanks to him, the right to celebrate Christmas has been restored to the people of Cuba. Unfortunately, the Cuban government has shown no interest in restoring other freedoms. On the contrary, authorities have been heavy-handed in crushing efforts to express dissent or to mobilize support for internationally recognized human rights.

It is the responsibility of the United States, our partners in the hemisphere, and the world at large to maintain pressure for democratic change. To this end, the Clinton Administration will continue to support adequate funding for broadcasting to Cuba. We will ask the Broadcasting Board of Governors to study possible additional broadcasting sites, and we will intensify our efforts through public diplomacy to promote international support for those in Cuba who are struggling to gain the freedoms to which people everywhere are entitled.

As President Clinton emphasized in his own statement today, our policy is designed to promote closer ties between our people and those of Cuba without providing aid and comfort to a repressive and backward looking regime. Our policy recognizes the importance of helping Cuban families to overcome the divisions imposed by immigration and exile. For as one Cuban American leader told us, in building civil society the strongest non-governmental organization is the family.

Before closing, I want to note with appreciation the constructive proposal put forward by Senators Warner and Dodd and others concerning the possible creation of a bipartisan commission on U.S. policy towards Cuba. Although we do not support establishing such a commission at this time, we will continue to work with them and others on constructive ideas for encouraging a democratic transition in Cuba.

Next year, the world will begin a new century. In Cuba, where the population is especially young, the personalities and policies, the leadership remained mired in the past but the focus of the people is rightly on the future. We and the people of Cuba must act with tomorrow in mind. Fully aware of present obstacles, we share a faith in the power of liberty to inspire peaceful but far-reaching change. Although we cannot foretell how soon, we know the day is drawing closer when the community of freedom will once more encompass the pearl of the Antilles, and the hemisphere of the American democracies will be complete.

Thank you very much.

FACT SHEETS ON U.S.-CUBA POLICY INITIATIVES

RELEASED BY THE BUREAU OF INTER-AMERICAN AFFAIRS,
U.S. DEPARTMENT OF STATE

January 5, 1999

Direct Flights

U.S. Policy

On January 5, 1999, the President announced his decision to expand direct passenger charter flights to Cuba.

As the President has said, we want to continue to find ways to support the Cuban people without strengthening the regime. Our objective, building on the visit of the Pontiff to Cuba, is to support the development of peaceful independent activity and civil society in order to help the Cuban people prepare for a transition to a free, independent, and prosperous nation.

New Measures

In addition to the existing licensed direct passenger charter flights to Havana from Miami, departures from some other U.S. cities will be authorized. In order to facilitate the licensed travel of individuals whose relatives live outside of Havana, direct flights will also be authorized to Cuban cities other than Havana.

The Departments of the Treasury, Commerce, and State will develop implementing procedures in the coming weeks, and will continue to license qualified carrier service providers.

Background

The United States is expanding direct passenger charter flights as a way to facilitate family reunification and to promote people-to-people exchanges through licensed travel.

This will promote the development of peaceful independent activity and civil society within Cuba.

Travelers on all flights must be licensed. In addition to persons traveling once a year to visit close relatives, by far the largest category, other licensable travel includes persons traveling for clearly defined religious or educational activities, cultural activities, persons belonging to recognized human rights organizations and other non-governmental groups, journalists, and official U.S. government travelers, among others.

Direct Mail

U.S. Policy
On January 5, 1999, the President announced his decision to seek to re-establish direct mail service with Cuba.

As the President has said, we want to continue to find ways to support the Cuban people without supporting the regime. Our objective, building on the visit of the Pontiff to Cuba, is to support the development of peaceful independent activity and civil society in order to help the Cuban people prepare for a transition to a free, independent, and prosperous nation.

New Measures
The U.S. government will contact the Cuban government to work out the details of establishing direct mail service.

Background
Direct mail between the United States and Cuba is authorized by the Cuban Democracy Act of 1992. It was suspended in 1962.

Currently mail is sent to and from Cuba via third countries, causing significant delays and sometimes losses.

Establishing direct mail will facilitate people-to-people contacts, and will significantly expand the flow of information to the Cuban people.

Food Sales

U.S. Policy

On January 5, 1999, the President announced his decision to authorize licensing of sales of food and agricultural inputs to independent entities in Cuba.

As the President has said, we want to continue to find ways to assist and support the Cuban people without strengthening the regime. Our objective, building on the visit of the Pontiff to Cuba and following up on the measures we announced last March 20, is to promote the development and evolution of peaceful independent activity and civil society. This will help promote a transition to a free, independent, and prosperous nation, and will help prepare the Cuban people for that goal.

New Measures

—Licensing, on a case-by-case basis, sales of food to entities independent of the Cuban government. This could include religious groups, private restaurants, and other such entities.

—Licensing, on a case-by-case basis, the sales of agricultural inputs to entities independent of the Cuban government. This could include private farmers, farmers in cooperatives raising food for sale in private markets, and other such entities.

U.S. government financing for such exports will not be authorized.

The Departments of Commerce, the Treasury, and State will develop licensing procedures in the coming weeks.

Background

Sales of food and agricultural inputs were suspended in 1963.

Sales to independent entities and non-governmental organizations will be licensed as a way to promote the development of activity independent of the government in order to encourage a peaceful democratic transition.

The embargo remains in place, except for licensed activity, and will continue to be enforced.

Appendixes

Increased Public Diplomacy

U.S. Policy
The United States has an active public diplomacy effort around the world focusing on the deplorable human rights situation in Cuba.

As the President has said, we want to continue to find ways to support the Cuban people without supporting the regime, and to support the development of peaceful independent activity and civil society. The United States will intensify efforts to bring the reality of Cuba to the attention of the world public opinion and world governments.

New Measures
USIA will study alternative broadcast sites in order to try to improve reception of Radio Martí and TV Martí.

We will be seek to identify funding for a new aerostat for TV Martí broadcasts to Cuba.

A new Presidential Advisory Board on Broadcasting to Cuba will be named.

USIA and State Department will enhance public diplomacy programs to better inform Latin America and the EU countries on the reality of Cuba today.

Increased People-to-People Contacts

U.S. Policy
On January 5, 1999, the President announced his decision to expand people-to-people contacts.

As the President has said, we want to continue to find ways to support the Cuban people without strengthening the regime. Our objective, building on the visit of the Pontiff to Cuba, is to support the development of peaceful independent activity and civil society in order to help the Cuban people prepare for a transition to a free, independent, and prosperous nation.

New Measures

We wish to encourage an expansion of educational, cultural, humanitarian, religious, journalistic and athletic exchange, and other appropriate people-to-people contacts. For example, the Baltimore Orioles organization will be licensed to explore the possibility of playing exhibition games where profits would benefit Caritas-Cuba.

These people-to-people contacts will be expanded in two ways: by facilitating travel of persons from Cuba to the United States who qualify for visas; and by streamlining licensing procedures for qualified U.S. persons traveling to Cuba.

Travel from Cuba to the United States:

—Qualified Cubans who are not senior members of the Cuban government or party will continue to be given visas.

—The visa process will be streamlined and accelerated.

Travel to Cuba from the United States:

—Licensing procedures will be streamlined for qualified U.S. persons traveling to Cuba.

—We will also develop procedures to license multiple visits for qualified individuals and groups in the above-mentioned categories.

—Travel for recreation or tourism, or travel otherwise in contravention of the embargo, continues to be prohibited.

The Departments of Treasury, Justice, and State will develop licensing procedures.

Background

Expanding educational, cultural, journalistic, athletic, religious and humanitarian exchanges to and from Cuba will facilitate people-to-people contacts, specifically supporting the development of peaceful activities in Cuba independent of the Cuban government and promoting a peaceful transition to democracy.

The revised visa procedures are not intended to expand contacts or relations between the U.S. and Cuban governments. Visa applications by senior-level Cuban officials will continue to be reviewed in Washington on a case-by-case basis.

Remittances

U.S. Policy

On January 5, 1999, the President announced his decision to expand legal remittances to the Cuban people.

As the President has said, we want to continue to find ways to support the Cuban people without strengthening the regime. Our objective, building on the visit of the Pontiff to Cuba, is to support the development of peaceful independent activity and civil society in order to help promote a transition to a free, independent, and democratic state.

New Measures

Under a general license, any U.S. citizen will be authorized to send up to $300 each quarter of the year to any Cuban family, except for senior-level Cuban government and communist party officials. Cuban Americans will continue to be permitted to send remittances to family members.

Remittances may be sent for humanitarian purposes, i.e., to support Cuban families.

U.S. citizens and non-governmental organizations will be licensed, on a case-by-case basis, to send larger remittances to entities in Cuba that are independent of the Cuban government.

The Departments of the Treasury and State will develop licensing and monitoring procedures.

Background

Legal remittances by Cuban Americans to close family members in Cuba for humanitarian purposes were reinstituted in March 1998.

Many Cubans are able to meet the most basic necessities of life for their families only by receiving humanitarian packages and financial assistance from relatives in the United States.

Expanding remittances helps promote greater individual freedom. Recipients will be less dependent on the state and less subject to its economic pressures.

Expanding remittances beyond close family members of Cuban Americans to other Cubans helps them for humanitarian purposes, reduces their dependence on the State and promotes independent civil society.

1998 REPORT ON THE CUBAN THREAT TO U.S. NATIONAL SECURITY

DEFENSE INTELLIGENCE AGENCY

November 18, 1997

This report has been prepared by the Defense Intelligence Agency in coordination with the Central Intelligence Agency, the Department of State Bureau of Intelligence and Research, the National Security Agency, and the United States Southern Command Joint Intelligence Center pursuant to Section 122B of Public Law No. 105-85, 111 Stat. 1943–44, November 18, 1997.

Cuban Armed Forces Significantly Weakened
The disintegration of the Soviet bloc in 1989 triggered a profound deterioration of the Cuban Revolutionary Armed Forces (FAR), transforming the Institution from one of the most active militaries in the Third World into a stay-at-home force that has minimal conventional fighting ability.

—The end of Soviet economic and military subsidies forced Havana to cut the military's size and budget by about 50 percent after 1989.

—In 1989 Cuba was the largest Latin American military on a per capita basis. Today the FAR is estimated to have about 50,000 to 65,000 regular troops and is comparable on an active duty per capita basis to countries like Colombia, Bolivia, Ecuador, and El Salvador.

—Severe resource shortages have forced the FAR to reduce training significantly.

—A substantial portion of the FAR's military heavy equipment is in storage. Cannibalization of equipment is used to sustain active duty equipment and make up for shortages of spare parts.

Economic support and sustainment tasks have become as important as protecting the national territory, further weakening the FAR's conventional capabilities.

—The FAR must now grow its own food and raise money to pay for some of its own expenses. Significant numbers of active duty forces are devoted to agricultural, business, and manufacturing activities that help feed the troops and generate revenues.

—The military has also increased the level of economic and social services it provides to the civilian sector. The FAR now supplies more construction, engineering, manufacturing, health, and transportation services than it did in past years.

—These tasks diminish conventional military training efforts and further weaken the FAR's conventional capabilities.

Residual Strengths
The FAR retains some residual combat support strengths that are essentially defensive in nature.

—The military's intelligence and counterintelligence systems directed at the United States appear to have suffered little degradation. Cuba has shared intelligence with other countries including U.S. adversaries.

—Cuba has an agreement with Russia which allows Moscow to maintain a signals intelligence facility at Torrens also known as Lourdes which is the largest such complex outside the Commonwealth of the Independent States.

—Cuba's military early warning radar systems are aging but remain generally intact.

—The military leadership is combat-experienced and disciplined.

Army
The ground forces remain primarily armor and artillery units. Their readiness level is low due to severely reduced training.

—The FAR generally is not capable of mounting effective operations above the battalion level.

—Most equipment is in storage and unavailable on short notice.

Navy
The Navy has no capability to sustain operations beyond its territorial waters and focuses on defense of the Cuban coast.
—Cuba no longer has any functioning submarines in its inventory.
—Perhaps a little over a dozen of its remaining surface vessels are combat capable.
—The Navy retains a weak antisurface warfare capability using fast attack boats that carry STYX surface-to-surface anti-ship missiles. The Navy also retains an extremely weak antisubmarine warfare capability. The Cuban Navy can pose a more substantial threat to undefended civilian vessels.

Air Force
The Air and Air Defense Forces are now incapable of defending Cuban airspace against large numbers of high-performance military aircraft. Slower or less sophisticated aircraft, however, would be vulnerable to Cuban air and air defense systems.
—The Air Force probably has less than 2 dozen operational MiG fighters.
—Pilot training is judged barely adequate to maintain proficiency.
—Fighter sorties have declined significantly in recent years.
—Cuba would rely on its surface-to-air missiles (SAM) and its air defense artillery to respond to attacking air forces.

Special Operations Forces
Cuba's special operations units are smaller and less proficient than they were a decade ago, but they can still perform selected military and internal security missions.
—The FAR retains a battalion-size airborne unit and other special operations forces.
—Special operations training continues, albeit on a smaller scale than in the past.

Unconventional Forces
Cuba's paramilitary units—the Territorial Militia Troops, the Youth Labor Army devoted to agricultural production, and the naval militia—have suffered considerable degradation of morale and training over the last seven years. However, their core personnel still have the potential to make an enemy invasion costly.

Negligible Conventional Military Threat to the United States
Cuba's weak military poses a negligible conventional threat to the United States or surrounding countries.
—The Cubans almost certainly calculate that any attack on U.S. territory or forces would draw a swift, forceful U.S. reaction.
—Cuba could theoretically threaten small, undefended countries in Latin America. However, such action would run counter to its efforts in recent years to improve relations with neighboring countries. There are no current indications that Cuba would undertake any such action.

Biological Warfare Threat
Cuba's current scientific facilities and expertise could support an offensive BW program in at least the research and development stage. Cuba's biotechnology industry is one of the most advanced in emerging countries and would be capable of producing BW agents.

Threat of Mass Migration Currently Low
The threat of another government-sanctioned mass migration from Cuba is assessed as low as long as domestic political conditions remain stable.
—The 1994 accord indefinitely permits 20,000 Cubans per year to enter the United States, the largest legal annual number since the U.S. airlifts of 1965–1971. The Cuban government uses such a safety valve to help minimize social tension prompted by the poor economy.

—The 1995 accord, which provides for the return of illegal migrants to Cuba, also deters many Cubans from leaving unlawfully. The perception by the Cuban populace that Washington can and will repatriate most illegal migrants has sharply reduced the flow of rafters and will remain a key determinant of migration volume.

—Moreover, mass illegal migration discourages tourism and foreign investor confidence, two factors that Havana—now dependent on dollars from abroad—urgently needs to keep its economy afloat.

Nonetheless, pressures for migrants to flee to the United States despite Cuban and U.S. prohibitions would increase substantially if Cuba's economy—currently growing slowly—resumed a downward spiral, if the government was perceived to relax its position on illegal departures, or in the event of sustained political upheaval.

Potential for Internal Strife

The prospects for widespread civil unrest in Cuba that involves U.S. citizens, residents, or armed forces currently appear to be low.

—There is undoubtedly widespread desire for greater economic and political freedom and weariness with continuing hardship, deprivation and repression. Nonetheless, relatively few Cubans now appear willing to risk the consequences of pressing for sweeping political changes.

Over the long term, stability is likely to depend on the circumstances under which Castro leaves the scene. Pressures for change are likely to grow that the regime may find difficult to manage.

Threat of Attacks on U.S. Citizens and Residents

Cuban attacks on U.S. citizens or residents while they are engaged in peaceful protest in international airspace or waters currently appear unlikely.

During exile commemoration ceremonies since Cuba shot down two unarmed U.S. aircraft in international airspace in February 1996, the Cuban government has acted with restraint.

Conclusions

At present, Cuba does not pose a significant military threat to the United States or to other countries in the region. Cuba has little motivation to engage in military activity beyond defense of its territory and political system.

Nonetheless, Cuba has a limited capability to engage in some military and intelligence activities which would be detrimental to U.S. interests and which could pose a danger to U.S. citizens under some circumstances.

STATEMENT AT THE OCCASION OF THE SIGNING INTO LAW OF CUBAN LIBERTY AND DEMOCRATIC SOLIDARITY (LIBERTAD) ACT OF 1996 BY PRESIDENT WILLIAM J. CLINTON

RELEASED BY THE WHITE HOUSE OFFICE OF
THE PRESS SECRETARY

March 12, 1996

Today I have signed into law H.R. 927, the "Cuban Liberty and Democratic Solidarity (LIBERTAD) Act of 1996." This Act is a justified response to the Cuban government's unjustified, unlawful attack on two unarmed U.S. civilian aircraft that left three U.S. citizens and one U.S. resident dead. The Act imposes additional sanctions on the Cuban regime, mandates the preparation of a plan for U.S. assistance to transitional and democratically elected Cuban governments, creates a cause of action enabling U.S. nationals to sue those who expropriate or "traffic" in expropriated properties in Cuba, and denies such traffickers entry into the United States. It is a clear statement of our determination to respond to attacks on U.S. nationals and of our continued commitment to stand by the Cuban people in their peaceful struggle for freedom.

Immediately after Cuba's brutal act, I urged that differences on the bill be set aside so that the United States could speak in a single, strong voice. By acting swiftly—just 17 days after the attack—we are sending a powerful message to the Cuban regime that we do not and will not tolerate such conduct.

The Act also reaffirms our common goal of promoting a peaceful transition to democracy in Cuba by tightening the existing embargo while reaching out to the Cuban people. Our current efforts are beginning to yield results: they are depriving the Cuban regime of the hard currency it needs to maintain its grip on power; more importantly, they are empowering the agents of peaceful change on the island. This Act provides further support for the Administration's efforts to strengthen independent organizations in Cuba intent on building democracy and respect for human rights. And I welcome its call for a plan to provide assistance to Cuba under transitional and democratically elected governments.

Consistent with the Constitution, I interpret the Act as not derogating from the President's authority to conduct foreign policy. A number of provisions—sections 104(a), 109(b), 113, 201, 202(e), and 202(f)—could be read to state the foreign policy of the United States, or would direct that particular diplomatic initiatives or other courses of action be taken with respect to foreign countries or governments. While I support the underlying intent of these sections, the President's constitutional authority over foreign policy necessarily entails discretion over these matters. Accordingly, I will construe these provisions to be precatory.

The President must also be able to respond effectively to rapid changes in Cuba. This capability is necessary to ensure that we can advance our national interests in a manner that is conducive to a democratic transition in Cuba. Section 102(h), concerning the codification of the economic embargo, and the requirements for determining that a transitional or democratically elected government is in power, could be read to impose overly rigid constraints on the implementation of our foreign policy. I will continue to work with the Congress to obtain the flexibility needed if the United States is to be in a position to advance our shared interest in a rapid and peaceful transition to democracy in Cuba.

Finally, Title IV of the Act provides for the Secretary of State to deny visas to, and the Attorney General to exclude from the United States, certain persons who confiscate or traffic in expropriated property after the date of enactment of the Act. I understand that the provision was not intended to reach those coming to the United States or United Nations as diplomats. A categorical prohibition on the entry of all those who fall within the scope of section 401 could constrain the exercise of my exclusive authority under Article II of the Constitution to receive ambassadors and to conduct diplomacy. I am, therefore, directing the Secretary of State and the

Attorney General to ensure that this provision is implemented in a way that does not interfere with my constitutional prerogatives and responsibilities.

The Cuban regime's lawless downing of two unarmed planes served as a harsh reminder of why a democratic Cuba is vitally important both to the Cuban and to the American people. The LIBERTAD Act, which I have signed into law in memory of the four victims of this cruel attack, reasserts our resolve to help carry the tide of democracy to the shores of Cuba.

JOINT STATEMENT ON U.S.-CUBA
IMMIGRATION AGREEMENT

May 2, 1995

The United States of America and the Republic of Cuba have reached agreement on steps to normalize further their migration relationship. These steps build upon the September 9, 1994, agreement and seek to address safety and humanitarian concerns and to ensure that migration between the countries is safe, legal, and orderly.

Humanitarian Parole

The United States and the Republic of Cuba recognize the special circumstances of Cuban migrants currently at Guantánamo Bay. Accordingly, the two governments have agreed that the process of humanitarian parole into the United States should continue beyond those eligible for parole under existing criteria. The two governments agree that if the United States carries out such paroles, it may count them towards meeting the minimum number of Cubans it is committed to admit every year pursuant to the September 9, 1994, agreement. Up to 5,000 such paroles may be counted towards meeting the minimum number in any one year period beginning September 9, 1995, regardless of when the migrants are paroled into the United States.

Safety of Life at Sea

The United States and the Republic of Cuba reaffirm their common interest in preventing unsafe departures from Cuba. Effective immediately, Cuban migrants intercepted at sea by the United States and attempting to enter the United States will be taken to Cuba. Similarly, migrants found to have entered Guantánamo illegally will also be returned to Cuba. The United States and the Republic of Cuba will cooperate jointly in this effort. All actions taken will be consistent with the parties' international obligations.

Migrants taken to Cuba will be informed by the United States officials about procedures to apply for legal admission to the United States at the U.S. Interests Section in Havana.

The United States and the Republic of Cuba will ensure that no action is taken against those migrants returned to Cuba as a consequence of their attempt to immigrate illegally. Both parties will work together to facilitate the procedures necessary to implement these measures. The United States and the Republic of Cuba agree to the return to Cuba of Cuban nationals currently at Guantánamo who are ineligible for admission to the United States.

September 9, 1994, Agreement

The United States and the Republic of Cuba agree that the provisions of the September 9, 1994, agreement remain in effect, except as modified by the present Joint Statement. In particular, both sides reaffirm their joint commitment to take steps to prevent unsafe departures from Cuba which risk loss of human life and to oppose acts of violence associated with illegal immigration.

JOINT COMMUNIQUÉ ON U.S.-CUBA IMMIGRATION AGREEMENT

September 9, 1994

Representatives of the United States of America and the Republic of Cuba today concluded talks concerning their mutual interest in normalizing migration procedures and agreed to take measures to ensure that migration between the two countries is safe, legal, and orderly.

Safety of Life at Sea

The United States and the Republic of Cuba recognize their common interest in preventing unsafe departures from Cuba which risk loss of human life. The United States underscored its recent decisions to discourage unsafe voyages. Pursuant to those decisions, migrants rescued at sea attempting to enter the United States will not be permitted to enter the United States, but instead will be taken to safe haven facilities outside the United States. Further, the United States has discontinued its practice of granting parole to all Cuban migrants who reach U.S. territory in irregular ways. The Republic of Cuba will take effective measures in every way it possibly can to prevent unsafe departures using mainly persuasive methods.

Alien Smuggling

The United States and the Republic of Cuba reaffirm their support for the recently adopted United Nations General Assembly resolution on alien smuggling. They pledged their cooperation to take prompt and effective action to prevent the transport of persons to the United States illegally. The two governments will take effective measures in every way they possibly can to oppose and prevent the use of violence by any persons seeking to reach, or who arrive in, the United States from Cuba by forcible diversions of aircraft and vessels.

Legal Migration
The United States and the Republic of Cuba are committed to directing Cuban migration into safe, legal and orderly channels consistent with strict implementation of the 1984 joint communiqué. Accordingly, the United States will continue to issue, in conformity with United States law, immediate relative and preference immigrant visas to Cuban nationals who apply at the U.S. Interests Section and are eligible to immigrate to the United States. The United States also commits, through other provisions of United States law, to authorize and facilitate additional lawful migration to the United States from Cuba. The United States ensures that total legal migration to the United States from Cuba will be a minimum of 20,000 Cubans each year, not including immediate relatives of United States citizens. As an additional, extraordinary measure, the United States will facilitate in a one year period the issuance of documentation to permit the migration to the United States of those qualified Cuban nationals in Cuba currently on the immigrant visa waiting list. To that end, both parties will work together to facilitate the procedures necessary to implement this measure. The two governments agree to authorize the necessary personnel to allow their respective interests sections to implement the provisions of this communiqué effectively.

Voluntary Return
The United States and the Republic of Cuba agreed that the voluntary return of Cuban nationals who arrived in the United States or in safe havens outside the United States on or after August 19, 1994, will continue to be arranged through diplomatic channels.

Excludables
The United States and the Republic of Cuba agreed to continue to discuss the return of Cuban nationals excludable from the United States.

Review of Agreement
The representatives of the United States and the Republic of Cuba agree to meet no later than 45 days from today's announcement to review implementation of this Joint Communiqué. Future meetings will be scheduled by mutual agreement.

ADDITIONAL RESOURCES

The following documents are available on-line at the accompanying World Wide Web addresses.

Cuban Democracy Act of 1992 (Title XVII of H.R. 5006): Point browser to http://thomas.loc.gov/bss/d102query.html, and search for "H.R. 5006" under "Bill/Amendment Number." At next window click on "Text of Legislation." Drag down to "Title XVII."

Cuban Liberty and Democratic Solidarity (LIBERTAD) Act of 1996 (H.R. 927): http://frwebgate.access.gpo.gov/cgi-bin/useftp.cgi?IPaddress=162.140.64.21&filename=publ114.104&directory=/diskc/wais/data/104_cong_public_laws

Office of Foreign Assets Control, Cuban Assets Control Regulations: http://www.access.gpo.gov/nara/cfr/waisidx/31cfr515.html

Secretary of State Madeleine K. Albright, Opening Remarks on Cuba at Press Briefing followed by Question and Answer Session by other Administration Officials Washington, D.C., March 20, 1998: http://secretary.state.gov/www/statements/1998/980320.html

Fact Sheets prepared by the Office of the Coordinator for Cuban Affairs, Bureau of Inter-American Affairs, May 13, 1998:

Cuba Travel Violations: New Procedures for Fully Hosted Travelers: http://www.state.gov/www/regions/wha/fs_980513_cuba_travel.html

Implementing Procedures for Direct Humanitarian Cargo Flights: http://www.state.gov/www/regions/wha/fs_980513_cargo_flights.html

Implementing Procedures for Direct Passenger Charter Flights: http://www.state.gov/www/regions/wha/fs_980513_ charterflights.html

Implementing Procedures for Family Remittances to Cuba: http://www.state.gov/www/regions/wha/fs_980513_family.html

Implementing Procedures for Facilitating the Licensing of the Export of Commercially Sold and Donated Medicines, Medical Supplies and Equipment to Cuba: http://www.state. gov/www/regions/wha/fs_980513_medical_cuba.html

The Future of Transatlantic Relations (1999)
* †Robert D. Blackwill, Chairman and Project Director

* †*After the Tests: U.S. Policy Toward India and Pakistan* (1998)
Richard N. Haass and Morton H. Halperin, Co-Chairs; Cosponsored
by the Brookings Institution

* †*Managing Change on the Korean Peninsula* (1998)
Morton I. Abramowitz and James T. Laney, Co-Chairs; Michael J.
Green, Project Director

* †*Promoting U.S. Economic Relations with Africa* (1998)
Peggy Dulany and Frank Savage, Co-Chairs; Salih Booker, Project
Manager

* †*Differentiated Containment: U.S. Policy Toward Iran and Iraq* (1997)
Zbigniew Brzezinski and Brent Scowcroft, Co-Chairs

†*Russia, Its Neighbors, and an Enlarging NATO* (1997)
Richard G. Lugar, Chair

* †*Financing America's Leadership: Protecting American Interests and
Promoting American Values* (1997)
Mickey Edwards and Stephen J. Solarz, Co-Chairs

**Rethinking International Drug Control: New Directions for U.S. Policy*
(1997)
Mathea Falco, Chair

†*A New U.S. Policy Toward India and Pakistan* (1997)
Richard N. Haass, Chairman; Gideon Rose, Project Director

*Arms Control and the U.S.-Russian Relationship: Problems, Prospects, and
Prescriptions* (1996)
Robert D. Blackwill, Chairman and Author; Keith W. Dayton, Project
Director

†*American National Interests and the United Nations* (1996)
George Soros, Chairman

†*Making Intelligence Smarter: The Future of U.S. Intelligence* (1996)
Maurice R. Greenberg, Chairman; Richard N. Haass, Project Director

†*Lessons of the Mexican Peso Crisis* (1996)
John C. Whitehead, Chairman; Marie-Josée Kravis, Project Director

†*Non-Lethal Technologies: Military Options and Implications* (1995)
Malcolm H. Wiener, Chairman

---

*Available from Brookings Institution Press ($5.00 per copy). To order, call
1-800-275-1447.
†Available on the Council on Foreign Relations website at www.
foreignrelations.org.